HOW TO SET UP SPEAKING GIGS AND GET PAID

by Gini Graham Scott, Ph.D.

HOW TO SET UP SPEAKING GIGS AND GET PAID

Copyright © 2019 by Gini Graham Scott

All rights reserved. No part of this book may be used or reproduced by any means, graphic, electronic, or mechanical, including photocopying, recording, taping or by any information storage retrieval system without the written permission of the author except in the case of brief quotations embodied in critical articles and reviews.

TABLE OF CONTENTS

INTRODUCTION	5
CHAPTER1: DECIDING WHAT YOU WANT TO TALK ABOUT	7
Determining Your Audience	7
Determining Your Topic	8
Assessing Your Expertise, Authority, and Credibility	9
Creating a Website	10
Writing and Publishing a Book	10
Still Other Formats For Increasing Your Impact and Influence	11
Organizing the Material Supporting Your Talk	12
CHAPTER 2: ORGANIZING YOUR TALK OR PRESENTATION	15
Outlining Your Program	15
Determining the Materials and Equipment You Need	19
Checking Out the Technology to Make Sure Everything Works	20
Determining the Room Set-Up	21
Organizing Any Display and Promotional Materials	23
Making Arrangements to Record Your Presentation	26
Hiring a Videographer	26
Setting Up the Sign-In Table	28
Creating Sign-In Forms	30
Creating Handouts	33
Creating an Evaluation Form	35
Planning for Any Refreshments	37
Allowing Some Time for Networking	38
Creating a Checklist for Everything to Bring	38
CHAPTER 3: MAKING THE ARRANGEMENTS FOR YOUR TALK	40
Helping an Organization Set Up and Promote an Event	40
Getting Started in Setting Up Your Own Event	40
Deciding What to Charge Attendees	41
Deciding on the Date	41
Deciding on the Location	42
Determining the Costs for the Space You Rent	44
Booking the Venue for Your Event	45
CHAPTER 4: MARKETING AND PROMOTING YOUR TALK	49
Promoting Your Event for an Organization	49
Places to Market and Promote Your Event	49
Setting Up Your Event on Event and Meeting Platforms	50
Creating Promotional Flyers for Your Event	64
Creating a Flyer for Future Events	67
Announcing Your Event at Group Meetings	69

- Announcing Your Event on the Social Media 70
- Announcing Your Event on Your Website 71
- Getting Announcements in Your Membership Organizations 72
- Advertising Your Event to the Venue's Audience 73
- Setting Up a Table or Booth at a Local Trade Fair 74
- Contacting the Local Media 76

CHAPTER 5: PUTTING ON YOUR EVENT 79
- The Final Count-Down Before Your Event 79
- What to Do the Day of the Event 80
- It's a Set-Up 80
- Greeting Attendees and Networking 82
- Putting on Your Presentation 82
- After It's All Over 83

CHAPTER 6: DEVELOPING A PROMOTIONAL VIDEO FROM YOUR EVENT 84
- Getting Ready for the Video Shoot 84
- Planning the Edit 85
- Determining How to Cut Your Video 89

CHAPTER 7: USING YOUR FIRST EVENT TO GET OTHER GIGS 92
- Review Your Event to Improve for the Future 92
- Deciding What to Change 93
- Use Your Video to Promote Your Presentation 95
- Using Photos from Your Event in Your Promotional Materials 95
- Creating Promotional Materials 96
- Deciding Who to Pitch 104
- Creating a Database of Contacts 106
- Making Calls and Sending Out Your Pitches 106
- Hiring Help with Marketing and Promotion 108
- Finding the Help You Need for Marketing and Promotion 109
- Taking the Next Steps 110

ABOUT THE AUTHOR 111
OTHER AVAILABLE BOOKS ON INSPIRATION, MOTIVATION, AND SUCCESS 112

INTRODUCTION

I got the idea for *How to Set Up Speaking Gigs and Get Paid* as a result of my experience in transitioning from writing books and scripts for myself and clients to speaking on the topics of my books. Then, I used my first speaking gig as a basis to get more gigs with the help of a research assistant and marketing assistant.

The whole process began as the result of my getting an opportunity to do a two to three minute pitch about my work to two dozen women at a monthly gathering of Nexus Women, a group of women small business owners and professionals. I got the opportunity to make this pitch since I was one of two people who brought snacks and coffee for the group.

As it happened, the featured speaker was Barbara Edwards, a business coach and the former CEO of California Hosts, and she was impressed when she heard me talk about how I had written over 200 books and had written and produced 10 feature films and documentaries. As a result, we had a few meetings and she became something of a mentor to guide me on setting up my first speaking engagement. She said that the residents of Lafayette and surrounding cities should know about me as a "hidden gem" in their community. How? She urged me to begin speaking to individuals in the area. All I had to do was pick a topic, set up a speaking program at a venue in the area, and promote it. Then, she assured me people will come, and this will be a great way to get more clients once people knew about me. Or so we hoped.

In the meantime, I had already taken some classes a year before on creating a talk with Julia Glyde, a local coach, on speaking, creating videos, and gaining visibility. Additionally, I had already been doing some short presentations to local business referral and networking groups associated with the Chambers of Commerce in Danville, Pleasant Hill, Walnut Creek, and Lafayette. I had also done some informal talks with groups I set up through Meetup, a national organization that helps local coordinators set up all types of face-to-face meetings.

But I had never tried to create a program that I could use to attract paying attendees or pitch to organizations and corporations. So that's how my success secrets program began with some guidance from Barbara Edwards.

This book shows what I did and how you can create your own speaking program. This doesn't mean quit your job and create a career as a speaker. Rather, this book is designed to help you create a program doing speaking, workshops, online courses, and related programs you can do on the side -- perhaps a few times a month or once or twice a week. Also, you can turn your speaking into an online webinar program, based on turning your presentation into a series of videos with you speaking or possibly with PowerPoint slides. That's what I hoped to do, and after my first gig, I brought in a research and marketing assistant to help me – which you can do, too.

CHAPTER 1: DECIDING WHAT YOU WANT TO TALK ABOUT

A first step to launching your speaking program is deciding what you want to talk about and the potential audience for your talk. There has to be a good match of your topic and audience for you to ultimately be successful.

Thus, you first have to determine what your likely audience will be interested in and whether what you want to talk about will appeal to them. If not, either identify a different audience that will be interested in your subject or change your topic to fit your audience, as long as it's a topic where you have an expertise.

If you have different topics that appeal to different audiences, pick one to start, so you concentrate your efforts there. Then, after you have a successful first gig on that subject, you can move on to the next topic and audience.

Determining Your Audience

Determining your audience might be fairly easy, if you are already providing services or products to a particular market, and you want to speak to groups in that market space in order to get more clients and make money from your speaking.

For example, say you are a business coach or consultant. Your target market will be the business audience you have been consulting with, except now you want to get them to your speaking program. Or suppose you are a dog trainer and you want to speak about caring for dogs. Your target audience is individuals and families who own or plan to own a dog.

In my case, I thought about the books I had written on different topics, and I determined that my audience was largely professionals, business owners, and corporations interested in my main topics: success, publishing books, resolving conflicts, and becoming more creative to be more productive and profitable.

Now, take some time to determine your prospective audience and write down these audiences on the form below. Add more rows as needed. If you have more than one audience, rank them from one to however many you have listed, where 1 is the audience you most want to connect with, 2 is your next preferred audience, and so on.

Potential Audience	Areas of Interest	Ranking of Audience (1=top rank; 2=next rank; etc.)
1)		
2)		
3)		

Determining Your Topic

What do you want to talk about to your audience? You may have a general idea of the topic, but narrow it down and give each talk a compelling title, where you emphasize the benefits for whoever comes to hear you speak. In other words, think about your program from the audience member's perspective -- what are you offering that is new and valuable. Even if the topic is a common one -- such as how to be more successful in a particular field, consider what you can add to make your approach more unique, such as showing how you overcame a series of personal challenges to become the success you are now.

For example, here's how I created my own list:
1) Success Secrets in Everyday Life
2) Increase Your Impact and Influence
3) Resolving Conflicts with Others and in Yourself
4) Increasing Your Creativity to Be More Productive and Resolve Problems

A good way to pick your topic is to think of ways to provide tips to prospective clients in your field. If you have an interesting story about how you achieved your current success, you can use that to illustrate one or more of your tips. For example, one of my clients whose company remodeled homes created a book and talk on how to remodel anything in your home successfully. Another client who had observed multiple instances of corruption when she worked in several hospitals wanted to talk about how individuals can avoid many problems in getting health care and coverage.

Now create your own list of topics. Pick one to six topics and give them a working title. You can always change the title if you find a better one. Rank the topics in the order in which you want to focus on them.

Topic	Title	Rank
1)		
2)		
3)		
4)		
5)		
6)		

Assessing Your Expertise, Authority, and Credibility

Now that you know your topic and have identified your primary audience, consider your expertise, authority, and credibility. How can you show you are knowledgeable about that topic? Or how can you develop that expertise, authority, and credibility.

As a first step to showing your knowledge and credibility, think about any awards, testimonials, and media publicity you have gotten. Organize that material so you can use it in your promotion or publicity for your event or to get others to hire you as a speaker. If you don't already have testimonials, publicity clippings, or descriptions of awards, do some research to obtain this material, including reaching out to individuals to request testimonials.

You can use the following table to organize this material, and note where you have it or have to do research to get it. Add more rows as needed for each category.

Past Awards, Testimonials and PR		
	Have It	Where to Obtain Information
Awards		
Testimonials		
Publicity		

Creating a Website

You can add to your authority with a website, where you can post your bio, speaking topics, awards, testimonials, and publicity. You can also include videos, excerpts from books, articles, blogs, and other materials related to your topic. These postings help to provide you with a presence and show off your expertise.

Ideally, work with a professional web designer for the strongest Internet presence. There are also a number of free website services that enable you to create a website, though you may have to allow some advertising or pay a monthly hosting fee.

Writing and Publishing a Book

Another way to add to your authority is to publish a book. When you are starting out, especially if you are speaking about self-help or business topics, you are unlikely to find a traditional publisher. These publishers will generally want you to have a "platform," based on already having a following, such as many thousands of social media followers, national media coverage, and a large audience attending your speaking engagements.

But you don't need a traditional publisher. You can readily publish and promote your book through any of the major book publishing platforms, such as KDP (formerly CreateSpace) or Kindle. Then, since you are publishing a print on demand (POD) book, you can order as many books as you want and get them in a week to 10 days.

In order to publish, after you set up your account with the required bank and tax information, all you need is a completed PDF or Word document in the format you choose (6x9, 7x10, 8x10, 8 ½x11, or other size) and a front cover image.

To publish a digital Kindle edition, you just upload the Word document and front cover image, and within a day you can have this approved. To create a paperback through KDP, you need a PDF file for the interior, which you can create from your Word document, and a 300 dpi PDF front and back cover, or use a KDP template with your cover image. For more details on how to do this, I have written several books on self-publishing: *Self-Publishing Secrets, Self-Publishing Your Book in Multiple Formats,* and *A Guide to Self-Publishing Your Book in Multiple Formats.*

As for the interior content, many books today are around 50 to 100 pages, although your book can be as short as 24 pages to be published. Or you can write an even longer book.

To write your book, think of what you want to speak about and write your book to share your talk in written form or go into more depth on that topic. A typical book might be about how to do something or a narrative about your experiences in doing what you are doing, along with the lessons you learned along the way.

There are numerous ways to write your book, including the following:

- Turn a series of 5 or more blogs on that topic into a book.
- Create an outline for your book. Divide it into chapters, divide the chapters into sections, and write up each section.
- If you don't have the time, interest, or ability to write your book, you can talk into a recording device and have that transcribed. After that, edit your transcript to create the book.
- You can turn the whole project over to a ghostwriter who can work from your notes, journals, blogs, or do interviews with you. Many ghostwriters, including myself, can write about 50-60 pages a week, so the first draft of the book can be completed in a week or two. Allow another week for your feedback and corrections, followed by an editorial polish.

To create your cover, unless you are an artist, you can obtain photos and graphics from stock photo houses. There are also some sites that offer photos at no charge, though it's nice to tip the photographers or make a donation to the site. You can add text to the cover using a program like Photoshop. Another option for creating the cover is to outsource the design work to a designer. One service that offers multiple choices from dozens of designers is 99designs.com for about $300 to $500. Another source of designers for about $25 to $50 is a service called Fiverr.com. The costs are comparatively low because many of the designers come from countries with lower costs, such as Pakistan, Indonesia, Sri Lanka, and Nigeria. I've used both services for my clients and my covers with much success. If you work with a ghostwriter, the ghostwriter can coordinate your search for a cover designer.

Still Other Formats For Increasing Your Impact and Influence

Still another way to multiply your impact and influence is presenting your material in multiple formats. Besides articles, blogs, and books, you can readily make videos from PowerPoints, stock images, and video clips. Or make a video by using the video feature on your phone. You can also turn your material into an online course, create press releases, and write social media posts. You can even create your own radio show or podcast at no cost, using various platforms that host your material, such as BlogTalkRadio.com. Another possibility is doing guests posts for individuals doing blogs in your field or writing articles for local publications.

The advantage of using different formats is you can share your message with individuals who prefer to receive content in different ways -- from reading a book to listening to an audio presentation to viewing a video.

For more details about using these different formats, my book is *Increase Your Impact and Influence*.

Organizing the Material Supporting Your Talk

Once you have determined your topic or topics, organize all the materials you have developed on that subject. Besides using them in your presentation, you can use some materials in your PR, and you may be able to offer some items for sale at your presentations. You might also draw on these materials in preparing your talk, such as by turning sections into PowerPoints or incorporating quotes in your talk.

This is what I did after thinking about the key subjects I could talk about. As the following example shows, I listed all the books I had written on a particular topic, so I might draw from them in crafting my presentation or creating a sales display.

1) **Success Secrets in Everyday Life**
   Based on *Success Secrets in Everyday Life*
   Other books on success:
   Affirming Your Success
   More Success and Happiness
   20 Rhymes for Your Success
   Pursue Your Passion
   Control Your Thoughts, Control Your Life
   Find True Happiness
   Work It Right
   The Business Connection Game

2) **Increase Your Impact and Influence**
   Based on *Increase Your Impact and Influence*
   Other Books, based on sharing your message in multiple formats
   Conducting a Monthly Social Media Video Campaign
   Conducting a Monthly Social Media Campaign
   Self-Publishing Solution
   Self-Publishing Your Book in Multiple Formats
   Guide to Self-Publishing Your Book in Multiple Formats

3) **Resolving Conflicts with Others and In Yourself**
   Based on *Resolving Conflict*
   Related books:
   How to Turn Your Unhappy Clients into Happy Clients
   Dealing with Impossible Clients
   Work with Me: Resolving Everyday Conflict in Your Organization
   A Survival Guide for Working with Humans
   A Survival Guide for Managing Employees from Hell
   Using the Dog Type System for Success in Business and the Workplace

4) Increasing Your Creativity to Be More Productive and Resolve Problems
   Related books:
   Want It, See It, Get It
   Mind Power: Picture Your Way to Success
   The Empowered Mind: How to Harness the Creativity In You
   Turn Your Dreams into Reality
   Use Your Dreams to Develop Your Next Book, Creative Project, or Business Idea
   The Vision Board Book
   The Business Connection Game

Similarly, think of the materials you have developed in different formats for each topic. For example, you may have blogs, handouts, PowerPoints, videos, games, and other material you have already prepared or want to develop.

You can draw on those materials in developing your talk, and you may be able to sell some of these materials, such as books, after your presentation. Here's a chart you can use to think about the relevant materials you can include in your talk or market at your talk. Use one chart for each topic.

Materials to Include in My Talk			
Material to Include	Have	To Develop	Timeline for Development

CHAPTER 2: ORGANIZING YOUR TALK OR PRESENTATION

Once you know what you want to talk about, you can organize your presentation based on the time you have for your program. These programs generally fall into three main categories:
- an introduction to who you are or what you do,
- a keynote talk where you give a short presentation,
- a longer in-depth program.

The shorter programs sometimes include a chance for participants to interact with each other or experience visualization to imagine or experience something. But more typically experiential elements are included in the longer programs, and it is ideal to include them in the longer face-to-face programs. More specifically, these three types of programs are the following.

- 7-15 minutes -- an introduction to who you are and what you do. Typically, these are the introductory pitches you might do at a business referral or networking group. You might do an online introduction to your program to persuade people to sign up for more.

- 20-45 minutes -- a short introductory program featuring trends in your field or how-to tips. Commonly, such presentations are made at dinner meetings, luncheons, or organizational meetings, where you are a featured presenter. Sometimes these programs are used as short online webinars. Often these are free programs, though you may sometimes get a small honorarium for your presentation -- typically $50-100.

- 50-90 minutes - a program where you present your topic in more depth, and often the program may include participant interaction, games, or visualization to help attendees apply your message to their everyday life. While many speakers use free longer webinars or face-to-face programs to get prospects to sign up for a course, you can charge for these programs based on a per-participant fee or a program fee for the organization putting on your program.

Outlining Your Program

One way to think about creating your program is to consider it like outlining a book. You want to include a little about yourself, especially as it relates to your topic, plus include a little about your personal background to humanize you and make you more relatable. At the same time, think about how you can help others and create value for them. Even if you have great achievements, which add to your credibility and authority, keep the introduction short -- perhaps one to three minutes, since participants mainly want to know how you can help them.

For example, when I started developing my first paid speaking gig where I invited people to come to hear me, Barbara Edwards, who was mentoring me in this process, said that people would want to know how I had come to create so many books and films. They would want to hear about my life story and about the wide variety of books I had written, since she was impressed with what I did. So she planned to set the program up as an interview with me and asked me to write up a series of questions she could ask me about my story. Thus, initially, I planned to combine that interview with a PowerPoint I had created to introduce myself to some business networking groups I belong to.

But when I asked the events coordinator for the chamber of commerce which sponsored one of the business networking groups promoting my event, she told me: "People don't just want to hear about you. They want to know what you can do for them."

With that in mind, I recast my story to feature tips I learned along the way based on my experiences. As a result, I added in 25 slides with 100 tips, which turned into my *Success Secrets in Everyday Life* book and video. These books and videos then led me to think about how to expand this initial presentation into a workshop program based on individuals applying these tips in their workplace and in their relationships with others.

Think about your own project in a similar way. Besides telling your story of how you or your company came to do what you are doing now, focus on how your story, products, or services provide value to others.

Then, with that focus in mind, create an outline for your presentation and develop a rough timeline for how much time to devote to each section of your presentation, based on the total time you have. Creating slides for a PowerPoint presentation can help you set up the program, and these slides are ideal for highlighting the main topics you want to cover, though you don't have to use them if you can talk from short notes or a good memory.

The Elements to Include

Within the time limit for your program, you can incorporate various elements. Note on your outline when to introduce each element and how much time to devote to it. The elements you can include are these:

- A PowerPoint presentation with photos, graphics, text, and sometimes audio or video clips that features the main points you want to cover. The text can include a few words or phrases for each topic or complete sentences to make key points.
- A demonstration of the product or service
- A video showing the product or service in use
- Brochures or flyers (though it is best to pass them out after the program, so they don't distract participants from paying attention to you).

- Questions from participants
- Questions to preselected participants to respond when you call on them. You can print the questions on cards you give out to the participants in advance.
- An opportunity for participants to get into pairs or groups to discuss a topic. Then, a spokesperson for a few pairs or groups can report on the discussion.
- An interactive game in which participants move around and interact with each other about the subject of the presentation, such as in the *Business Connection Game*, where participants answer different questions as they move from table to table to join different groups.
- A visualization in which participants imagine themselves in various scenarios, such as achieving some goal or developing a new idea.
- An interview format in which someone interviews you using preselected questions to draw out your answers on a particular topic.

Creating Your Outline

With the time for your program in mind, decide on the elements to include and create your outline. You can list the different sections and topics in that section, or if you need help deciding what to include, discuss this with others participating in the presentation with you.

For example, in organizing my first speaking gig, Barbara and I had several discussions about how to structure the presentation. At this point, I had already expanded my PowerPoint about myself into *Success Secrets in Everyday Life* with 100 tips. At first I had thought to use that interview guide to talk about my life and the tips I learned from doing different things. Then, my outline would provide a guide for how much time to spend on each section. But Barbara suggested using an interview format in which she would interview me, and the *Success Secrets* PowerPoint, turned into a video, would go at the end. Additionally, I could include a video with the trailers of six feature films and documentaries I had created in the middle of the interview.

Thus, after we had two one hour meetings, the basic outline of the program emerged, based on us having 60 to 75 minutes for the program, aside from the networking:

1) About 15 minutes for arrivals and networking
2) A 2-minute introduction of me by the interviewer
3) About 20 minutes of an interview with me based on a series of questions.
4) About 12 minutes to show a video with six 2-minute film trailers.
5) Another 20 minutes of an interview with me
6) About 12 minutes to show the *Success Secrets* video
7) About 10 minutes for Questions and Answers from the audience
8) Another 15 minutes for networking after the presentation

Having an outline doesn't mean your program is set in stone, because you can change it as you decide on the content to include in the program. You may even need to make last minute changes due to contingencies that occur when you get ready to do the program. But creating an outline gives you a basic structure to guide you as you put your program together. Then, you can more closely work out what will go in each segment, much like laying out chapters in a book and deciding on the sections and subsections within each chapter.

For instance, since the plan was for Barbara to interview me, the next step was for me to write up a series of questions for her to ask and the answers I would give for each question. The reason for writing down the answers was not for me to remember them, since they would be hard to recall exactly, but to give Barbara a general idea of what I would say. Then, my written answers would help her ask follow-up questions, such as if I missed a key point in responding during the presentation.

Here's an example of the questions we decided to use that included my experiences and what I learned from them to share with others. I starred the questions I thought were less important, so Barbara could cut them if we ran out of time at the event.

1. How did you happen to write so many books?

2. What kind of process do you use to enable you to write so fast? Is this something that others can do?

3. If you end up turning your experiences into books, how do you decide which ones to develop?

*4. What is the latest project you are doing?

5. How did you start writing scripts?

6. How did you learn how to turn your scripts into films? How did you find people to be in your films? What groups did you join to learn about this?

7. How did your experience in producing films locally and going to Hollywood lead you to turn pro and produce feature films, documentaries, and TV series?

8. What kinds of books or scripts do you write for other people? How do you work with them?

*9. What experiences in your childhood led to what you are doing now?

10. What are the major challenges you face and how do you overcome them? What do you suggest to other people who are facing challenges in their life?

11. What is your guiding philosophy or goal in life?

12. You talk a lot of about using visualization in developing your books, films and other projects, and you have written about that process. How does that work?

13. When you are working on so many projects at the same time, how do you organize or prioritize them? What do you recommend that other people do?

14. How are you able to write about so many different topics? Why don't you specialize in a particular area?

15. What does it take to get published today? What is the advantage of finding a traditional publisher versus self-publishing? How do you help people do either?

16. If people want to write their own book, what do you suggest they do? You suggest people use multiple formats and platforms to share their message? How do they do this?

17. What are the new projects you are working on?

18. Where will you be presenting these programs?

19. How is what you are doing new and different compared to all of the speakers talking about success, motivation, self-help, and business topics?

Even if you don't want to use an interview format, creating a list of questions can help you think about what you want to talk about. Additionally, you can include a section where you talk about your plans for the future. Indicate if you are planning some future on-line or face-to-face programs, so participants can look forward to attending a future program with you.

Determining the Materials and Equipment You Need

Once you know what you want to say, determine the materials you need for your presentation. Later, you will consider the materials to promote and market your talk.

Some things you may need include the following. Select the items you want to include for each presentation:
- PowerPoint presentation file
- video files in mp4 format, possibly in different resolutions so you can show the highest resolution video (1080 pixels) if you can, but show a lower resolution video (720 or 480 pixels) if necessary
- a flash drive with your video or PowerPoint files
- your video uploaded on YouTube, Vimeo, or other hosting site along with a print-out of each link, in case you need to find the video to show at your presentation
- photos, illustrations, or charts
- one or more easels to show your photos, illustrations, or charts
- one or more binders for your materials
- cards with questions for participants
- game materials if you are including a game
- a laptop to show a video, PowerPoint, or documents on a screen (unless the venue for your presentation has a laptop you can use)
- a projector to connect a laptop to the screen (unless the venue for your presentation has a projector you can use)
- a cable with a VGA, USB or other connector to connect your laptop to the projector (unless the venue for your presentation has one).

Be sure that all your equipment works well. Also, time your presentation and practice giving it. Make sure you have everything needed to present your message so that you can deliver it smoothly to the audience.

Checking Out the Technology to Make Sure Everything Works

Check your equipment so you know how to use any technology or arrange to have someone to assist you for as long as needed to set up and handle the technology. Otherwise, things can go terribly wrong.

I discovered that at my first presentation. I planned to incorporate two videos in the program -- one in the middle of the interview to show the trailers for the films I wrote and produced, and one at the end to feature my *Success Secrets in Everyday Life* presentation with slides about myself, my books, and tips I had learned from my experience. I not only put MP4 files of each video with three resolutions on the flash drive but for backup, I uploaded the high resolution files of each video on YouTube. Additionally, a week before my presentation, I brought in my PowerPoint presentation, before I turned it into a video, to check out the connection with the screen. It was an old laptop with only a PowerPoint viewer, so some of the images appeared in different positions on the slide. But at worst, I figured I could use this laptop if the connection to YouTube didn't work. Thus, all I had to do was convert the PowerPoint into a video and insert the flash drive to show it, so all would be fine.

But then it turned out things really weren't so fine at all.

The first problem occurred when the two techs setting up the equipment tried to set up the links on the laptop to YouTube. Unfortunately, though I had printed out both video links, I couldn't find that document in the swirl of flyers and other papers I brought to the presentation. And my request to go to my Changemakers Publishing YouTube channel brought up an unfamiliar site. Rather than take the time to search for the video links, I pulled out my flash drive and pointed out the file for the first video. But after it appeared on the screen, I realized there was no music. At first I thought the problem might be the high 1080 pixel resolution. So we tried the 720 version and then the 480 version, but still no music. Unfortunately, as the techs now realized, we didn't have a player set-up on the system.

Thus, it was back to finding the videos on YouTube. But it was hard to type in the name on an unfamiliar laptop, and when the tech typed in "Success Secrets in Everyday Life," a series of unfamiliar video listings scrolled by until I suggested adding the full name of the video, "Success Secrets in Everyday Life with Music". Then the correct video finally appeared.

The original plan was to show the video with the film trailers first and show the other video at the end. So one tech helped us find the second video and set it up at the top of the recommended videos list at the right. Then, presumably, at the end of the interview, all someone had to do was click "Esc" to exit the first video and click on the second video.

But at the end of the presentation, when I went to click on the second video, the list of YouTube recommendations had changed, so the video was no longer there. Thus, we had to type in the name of the video to find it, and it took several minutes to get to the right YouTube channel. Meanwhile, as we struggled to find it, most of the audience disappeared.

In short, the presentation turned into a high tech nightmare. Thus, a big caution is to carefully check out all of the equipment you are going to use whether it's your own or you are using the equipment provided by someone else.

Determining the Room Set-Up

Another key to a successful presentation is having a good room set up.

If you are doing the program for an organization, find out what kind of room you will be in, the available seating, and the size of the audience to expect. Also, check if there is a screen or blank wall for projecting a PowerPoint or video. Otherwise you have to bring a screen, though usually the organization will have one.

If you are doing the presentation in a venue you arrange, select a room to accommodate the number of participants you think is likely and arrange the seating accordingly.

It's also important to look around the room to make sure there won't be anything to detract from your presentation, such as pictures on the walls or equipment in the front of the room. Then, if necessary, arrange to have any distracting items removed or cover them up if possible, or find another venue if such efforts do not work.

I didn't think to carefully check the room myself, and the results could have been a disaster. Though I carefully imagined where the tables and chairs would go when I checked the room, I didn't notice the two sinks with faucets on a long counter in the front of the room. I didn't even notice them when I first arrived at the event and set up the sign-up tables and display tables. I only discovered them after the videographer had set up his equipment and said I wouldn't have a "visually pleasing" background for filming my presentation, since I would have the sink faucets right behind me. What could we do? I even considered driving back to my house, only five minutes away, to get some black table covers. But it was important for me to be there for set-up, and fortunately, I had a large brown blanket in my car that could cover up the faucets and sinks. It wasn't the best background, but at least the crisis was averted. The experience demonstrated the importance of carefully checking out the venue in advance.

Generally, for most presentations, figure on a classroom set up, with about 8 to 10 seats per row, though sometimes a set-up with rows of tables with chairs behind them works best if participants plan to write on laptops or access the Internet. If it's a small group, perhaps set up the seating in a circle or around a conference-style table.

If you have things to display, if possible, set up one or two six-foot tables on either side of the room.

Unless the organization where you are presenting your program is taking care of this, set up a sign-in table, where people can sign in as they arrive and pick up any flyers or promotional material you have to give out. It's best if you can position the table by the door where attendees arrive, so they don't have to walk across the room to get to the sign-in table. If you have two entrances and one table, ideally direct all arrivals to a single door, perhaps with a sign indicating which door to use.

If you have a drawing for a prize or raffle, set up a container for people to place business cards or have a stack of cards and a pen, so people without business cards can use these cards to sign in. If you are doing a raffle, obtain a roll of raffle tickets, so whoever is handling the raffle can tear off one ticket to place in the container and give the matching ticket to each participant.

Generally, plan to arrive 30 minutes in advance to set up everything before participants arrive. Some people may come as early as 10 to 15 minutes before the program, so it is best to have everything set up before anyone arrives.

For example, for my first speaking gig in a meeting room at the Lafayette Library, I discussed setting up the room with the Rental Room Coordinator. After she showed me the room, I decided to use five tables -- one for sign-ins, another for refreshments, a third with two chairs for the presentation, and two tables placed side by side for a display. The Coordinator also arranged to set up 20 classroom-style chairs and provide a projector and laptop. The layout looked something like this:

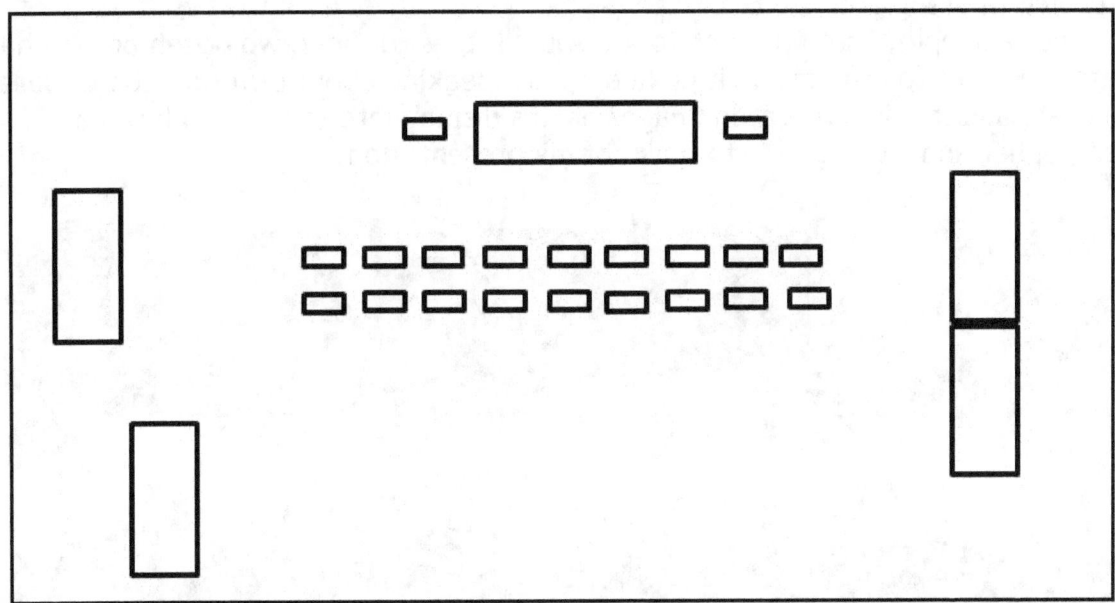

Likewise, you can map out your own layout for tables and chairs to help you design your room set-up. If someone else sets up the room and you can provide your input, this layout will help them know how to arrange it.

Organizing Any Display and Promotional Materials

Other materials to bring to your presentation include display and promotional materials, to be discussed in the next chapter.
The particular display materials will depend on your topic. These might include:
- product samples if your talk is based on products you represent,
- photos of you providing the service, if you offer a service,
- certificates, plaques, and awards you received.
- published books in your field.

If you plan to have back or front of the room sales after your presentation, include those in your display. In short, think of anything physical related to your presentation that you might display and decide what to bring, based on the space allowed for your display.

Additionally, you can use the sign-in table to display a few items. Usually, the best items to display here are flyers about future programs and special offerings for attendees. You can provide copies of any handouts here, unless you plan to hand them out during the program.

For example, I set up two 6 foot display tables to show two dozen books I had created in order to promote writing books and speaking about different topics based on my books. Later, I incorporated images of this display into the video I hired a videographer and video editor to make of my presentation.

To help you decide what to bring, you can use the following form to list all of the items you want to display. Add additional lines if you need more space.

Display and Promotional Items to Bring	
Products to Display	Number and Comments
Flyers to Display	Number and Comments

Making Arrangements to Record Your Presentation

Recording your presentation is a good idea if you want to use it to get future gigs. It doesn't matter if you have a small turnout. You can still record yourself doing the presentation without showing the audience. Then, you can use the video to show prospects who might want to have you speak to their group, since they often want to see an example of you doing a program. Usually a professional video is the way to go -- just capturing your talk on your phone is not enough.

If you are doing the presentation for an organization, get permission to record. Also, find out if the videographer will need any special cables or lights to set up the recording. If you are making your own room arrangements, check on what the videographer will need to do in order to record.

If you expect to record the audience, let people know before the meeting that you will be recording, so anyone who doesn't want to be in the video can move to a location where they won't be in the shot. Alternatively, indicate that you plan to record when people sign-up for the event. Then, unless the person lets you know verbally or by signing an opt-out form that they don't want to be in the video, they have given their consent to be recorded.

If you get a large enough turn-out, say at least 10 to 15 attendees, the videographer can record the audience. Ideally, get some shots when everyone is listening attentively, participating in break-out events in pairs or small groups, or otherwise showing they are enthusiastically engaged in your talk.

If you only have a small turnout, the videographer can skip recording the audience. So a low turn-out doesn't matter. What's important is that you give a good presentation and the videographer records that.

If you have a display, the videographer can record that, too, before or after your presentation. The videographer can do this with a long-shot to take in the whole display or do a pan shot, close-ups, or medium shots to show the items in your display more closely. For example, the videographer I hired filmed my book display by panning his camera along each row to feature each book for a second or two.

Hiring a Videographer

Where do you find a videographer to film your program and what should you expect to pay? There are a number of possibilities, and the cost can range from about $50 to $1000, with $200 to $300 the average. Based on an hourly rate, costs range from about $50 to $150 an hour, with $75 to $100 the average. Figure on a minimum of two hours, which includes a half-hour for set up, another half-hour for packing up, and one hour to film your presentation.

The costs vary widely based on the experience of the videographer. If a videographer is just starting out or is a high school senior or college student filming videos on the side, the cost might be $50 to $100. If you hire a video production company doing business videos, the cost will be much higher, about $750 to $1000. Freelance videographers charge somewhere in the middle.

In addition to the cost of the onsite filming, figure on an hour or two for editing. This can include adding opening titles, credits, contact information, and a few slides to introduce different sections of the video, such as before a video of a PowerPoint presentation or a display of your products. That's what I did when I included a 12 minute video trailer of six films I wrote and produced and a 12 minute Success Secrets video featuring slides about my background, books, and tips for success.

One typical arrangement is to pay the videographer the full amount when they arrive to do the shoot, along with an advance payment for editing. Another common practice is to pay one-third to one-half down to hold the date. If you pay one-third down, you might pay another third on the videographer's arrival and the final payment after the editing is completed. If you pay one-half down, you might make the rest of the payment for the video shoot and editing when the videographer arrives, or pay for the shoot and later pay the final amount due after editing.

The videographer will generally request one of these arrangements or you can negotiate the amount and payment arrangements at the time you hire the videographer. In some cases, a videographer or video company may ask for the full payment upfront, but I don't recommend this, because you risk making a payment and then the videographer doesn't show up or you don't like their work. If you have already paid in full, you may find you have little leverage to fix the problem or get a refund.

To decide on a videographer, look at some examples of what they have done. Most videographers will have a website featuring examples of their past work. These examples can help you decide if the videographer's style is a good match for you.

To find a videographer, here are a number of possibilities:
 - local business referral and networking groups
 - your local Chamber of Commerce
 - a search on Google for your area
 - a referral from a neighborhood online forum, such as Next Door, in response to a posting by you
 - checking online gig services, such as Upwork, Fiverr, and Thumbtack, for local videographers
 - contacting the career centers at local high schools and colleges to place a listing.

Select the types of contacts that make the most sense for you.

In my case, I originally hoped to hire a woman I met through a local business networking group, since she had been praised highly by several people who had hired her. However, she was selling her house and possibly moving, so that didn't work.

Next, I tried posting my request on my neighborhood Next Door forum, with no response.

Then, I contacted two videographers who were members of a business referral group. While one had no time, the other videographer who owned a video production company offered to do it, but his $750 cost was too high, and when I told him my budget of $300, he said one of his employees would do it. But when he sent me a detailed 5-page contract, it required a non-refundable payment in advance. I wrote back saying I wasn't comfortable with that.

After that, about a week before the program, I wondered if I should keep trying to find a videographer, since now there were only three paid sign-ups through Eventbrite, and Barbara suggested cancelling the program. But since 10 other people had signed up, though without paying, through a Success Secrets Meetup group I started, and other people could still sign up due to Chambers of Commerce and library newsletter announcements about the event. So I decided to press on, even if there was a low turnout, since I could still use the video to pitch my speaking programs.

And this time I found the videographer through a search for "videographers near me" in Google. One of the services advertising there was Thumbtack, which connects prospective employers to all kinds of services. When I checked out Thumbtack, I saw a few videographers listing various price points, and I found one in my $300 budget range. So I wrote to him, and within a few hours, he responded, and I checked out some of his past videos on his website. A few hours later, I offered him the job. Just pay in full at the event, he asked, which I thought was the ideal arrangement. A few minutes later he sent me a confirmation letter about the amount to pay, and after I wrote back that this was fine, he asked for details about the event location, what time to arrive to set up, and how the presentation would go. This way he could plan accordingly.

Though I found a videographer a week before the program, ideally make these arrangements two or three weeks or even a month in advance. This way you have plenty of time to select a videographer and work out the arrangements for filming your program.

Setting Up the Sign-In Table

If you are speaking to an organization that is handling the sign-in arrangements, you don't have to deal with this, although you may want to have some of your materials on the table. These materials might include information about future programs you are planning, a sign-up form to join your mailing list, information about your products or services, and your business card or small postcard with information about you.

If this is your own event, use your own check-in form. One approach is to have a list or printout of everyone who has prepaid, such as provided by Eventbrite or Meetup. Then, when people arrive, you check them off.

What if people arrive who haven't paid? If you can accept last-minute arrivals and collect payments at the door, be prepared to do this. Generally, at most venues, you can collect money at the event, though occasionally, some organizations may not permit you to accept money, so confirm that collecting money is allowed. If not, advise prospective attendees that they have to pay in advance, since no payments will be collected at the door. Alternatively, find another venue where you can collect money.

Assuming you are collecting money, bring a cash box for any cash, checks, or credit card information you receive. If you need to buy a cash box, you can get one at a local or online supply store, such as Office Depot, for about $20-40. In case people paying cash need change, place about $40-50 in $1, $5, and $10 bills in the cash box, depending on the denominations you are likely to receive. For instance, if the cost is $10, have some $10 bills for change if people pay you $20. If the cost is $15, have some $5 bills for change. Or have $1 bills if needed for change.

Should people pay by check, be sure there is a phone number on the check or ask for one, and make sure the check is signed. If not, ask the person to sign it.

If you can accept credit cards, bring a credit card processor or have a form to write down the credit information, so you can later enter it. To make sure this credit card information is correct, look at the person's credit card and enter the information yourself or verify that the person is filling in this information correctly. The information should include the card number, expiration date, and security code. Additionally, ask for the person's phone number and email in case you have any problem charging the card.

Also, provide a sign-up form where you can indicate which people are paying at the door, how much, and in what form they have paid you. This form can include the name of the people who have already paid, and you can check them off as they arrive. Additionally, provide a few pens so people can easily sign in. If you expect a large group, have a sheet with peel-off name tags, so people can wear these to help them mix with others at the event.

For example, next to the cash box on the sign-in table, we had a sign-up form for everyone who attended, and behind the form, we attached an Eventbrite confirmation for each person who had paid, along with a print-out of the people who had signed up through Meetup but hadn't paid. As people arrived, Barbara, who was at the door, checked off their names on either sheet. As it turned out, everyone who came had already paid, and the Eventbrite confirmation included an email, so we didn't need to ask anyone to sign the sign-up form. In sum, preferably use a single sign-in form for everyone, so all the information about attendees is in the same place.

Creating Sign-In Forms

Besides having a form for everyone attending the program, the other two forms you might include are these:
- a form indicating an interest in future programs, if you have such plans,
- a form for anyone using a credit card to pay.

You can attach each form to a clipboard. While the form for attendees should be at the sign-in table, the others might be there when participants sign in, or you can pass them around later before, during, or after the program.

The Form for Attendees

The form for anyone attending the program should include the person's name, phone number, email, and an indication of how they have paid, such as if they paid through Eventbrite, Meetup, PayPal, cash, check, or credit card. If you have the receipt for their payment, such as from Eventbrite, Meetup, or PayPal, you can attach it to the clipboard, so you can easily verify if the attendee has paid.

Here's an example of such a form:

SUCCESS SECRETS IN EVERYDAY LIFE – OCT 1				
Name	Phone	E-Mail	Ebrite	Cash/Check/Credit Card

The Form for Future Programs

The form for future programs should list the future programs you have planned or might plan to assess the level of interest in attending. This information can help you decide whether to put on a planned program or a program you have considered doing. If you have already scheduled or planned a program for a particular date, include that date. If there is insufficient interest, you can always cancel the program. If you are merely thinking about a possible program, leave the date open or indicate that it is TBA (to be announced).

To help you decide on or schedule future events, ask for the person's level of interest in each program. If they are interested, ask them to include an email so you can let them know more about the event. Also, ask them to indicate the best times for them to attend events.

Here's an example of the form we used at the Success Secrets program.

INTERP IN FUTURE PROGRAMS (Besides Listed Dates Besides Currently Schedule Dates)				
Program	Date	E-Mail	Level of Interest 0-5	Best Times for Events (Indicate Days and Times)
The New Age of Aging	Nov TBA			
Increase Your Influence and Impact	Dec. 5			
What You Can Learn from Dogs	Jan. 6			
Increasing Your Creativity to Be More Productive, Develop New Ideas				
Resolving Conflicts with Others and within Yourself -- at Work and In Your Personal Life				
Other Success Topics of Interest (write down topics below)				

Credit Card Form

If you can take credit cards, either bring the equipment to process the card or obtain the information so you can process the card later. For later processing, it's best to put this information on a separate form, although we planned to use a column for this information on the sign-up form. We didn't need this since everyone prepaid, but it is better to create a separate form for credit card information, so you can keep this information confidential, whereas if it is on the sign-up form, others can see it when they sign in.

Use this credit card form to get the person's credit card number, expiration date, security code, and zip code. Also, ask for their phone number and email in case you have to contact them about any problems charging the card. Also, on the form, specify the amount you are charging for your program and the date.

For example, the Credit Card Form we used looked like this:

Credit Card Information	
Name	
CC Number	
Expiration Date	
Security Code	
Address	
Zip Code	
Phone Number	
Email	

Creating Handouts

You can create all kinds of handouts, based on your topic and your goals for your program. If you hope to attract attendees to future programs, include a handout for that. If you have products or services, describe them in a flyer or brochure. If you have product samples, you might give some out. Possibly print-out the PowerPoint slides in your presentation. If you have many slides, you can print 4 to 6 slides on a page.

You can put some flyers and handouts on the sign-in table or display table or distribute them before or after your program. Another option is providing these materials in multiple ways, such as having them on the sign-in and display tables, or handing out materials on the display table, too.

A key reason for giving out handouts is you give people something to take away from your program, so they remember you and might later want to buy or sign up for something you offer. For example, at the introductory Success Secrets program, one handout featured a future workshop that attendees could sign up for. Another featured available books on Amazon, including the *Secrets of Success in Everyday Life* book, which featured the slides with tips that was shown at the end of the presentation.

There's an example of the future workshop flyer on the following page. Likewise, if you are planning to have future programs, include a handout about that. Additionally, talk about your future plans at the end of your presentation to build interest in attending these events.

SUCCESS SECRETS IN EVERYDAY LIFE
with GINI GRAHAM SCOTT

Author of 200+ Books from Self-Help and Business to Novels and Kids Books. Writer/Executive Producer of 10 Films
Lafayette Resident for 5 Years

A Workshop on How to Apply These Secrets in Your Everyday Life

Date and Time TBA - Sign Up with Your Email to Receive Details
Lafayette Library, Art & Discovery Room, 3491 Mt Diablo Blvd.

Gini will also share her secret tips on how she was able to achieve so much and how you can do it, too, whatever your goals, hopes, and dreams in your work and personal life. The program will draw on Gini's career experiences of over 40 years and cover topics such as:
- Turning failure into success
- Getting new ideas from your experiences
- Setting and achieving goals
- Increasing your creativity
- Using visualization to map out your path to success
- Prioritizing what you really want to do

The workshop will include discussion, interaction with others, visualization techniques, plenty of time for questions, and more.

A Brief Bio:
Gini Graham Scott, Ph.D., CEO of Changemakers Publishing and Writing, is an internationally known writer, consultant, speaker, and workshop leader. Her recent books include *Increase Your Impact and Influence, Self-Publish Your Book in Multiple Formats*, and the *New World Neanderthals*. Her latest films include *The New Age of Aging; Me, My Dog, and I;* and *Rescue Me.* She has published 50+ books with major publishers and 150+ books through Changemakers Publishing on social trends, business, self-help, and for kids. She has worked with hundreds of clients as a ghostwriter for books and scripts, and is a communications strategist and consultant. Her website is www.changemakerspublishingandwriting.com.

Creating an Evaluation Form

To get feedback on your program and suggestions for improvements, create an Evaluation Form to give to participants. This will give you insights into how well participants liked the program and what they liked most and least. This way, you can adapt your program to be even better in the future.

While you can hand out an Evaluation Form when attendees first check in, it can easily get ignored because of the other paperwork participants obtain when signing in or from any handouts you distribute. So generally, it is best to give out these forms at the end of the program, before or after any Q&A.

When you design and later hand out these forms, explain why you want these evaluations, such as to improve the program in the future. In some cases, program organizers offer an incentive for filling out these evaluations, such as entering those filling out the form in a prize drawing or giving a small prize to everyone who fills out a form. Such a prize can take the form of a small item with your name and company name on it, such as a glass tumbler, business card holder, or water bottle holder. Another possibility is giving out a sample of your product, a $25 to $50 certificate for your services, a $10 to $20 Starbucks card, or a PDF of a book you have written. Generally, participants who fill out these forms will be more receptive to your presentation, so they want to help you in making it better.

However, if you have a small group and many people leave immediately after your presentation, so few remain for networking, it might be futile to hand out Evaluation Forms, since few participants, if any, will fill them out. For example, at the first Success Secrets meeting, there were less than a dozen participants. Two attendees said they had to leave early to drive 30 miles to get home, and most of the other attendees didn't want to stay for networking. So I didn't hand out any forms.

If you do create an Evaluation Form, a good way to do so is to have a few general open-ended questions for opinions and suggestions. Then include questions where attendees can simply rate, such as from 1 to 5, how much they liked or didn't like something in the program. You can also use this form to invite people who liked your program to write a testimonial. If any attendees do give you a testimonial or if you offer a prize for turning in a form, ask attendees to include their email so you can contact them about future programs or send their prize. Otherwise, make including a name optional, since some attendees prefer not to provide their names, particularly if offering negative criticism. Conversely, I have found that attendees who feel positive about your program and provide helpful feedback are likely to include their names.

Here's an example of what an evaluation form might look like.

PROGRAM EVALUATION

1. How would you rate your experience of this program on a scale of 0-10? ____

2. What did you most like about the program and why?

3. What didn't you like or would you change?

4. What else would you like to learn about this topic?

5. What would you expect to pay for a 2 hour workshop on this topic?
    $20_____
    $30_____
    $40_____
    $50_____

6. Anything else you would like to suggest or add?

7. If you liked this program, can we get a testimonial we can include in our promotional materials about it, along with your name, city, and any website link you would like to include.

8. Would you like to be added to our mailing list to receive our newsletter, articles on this topic, and information on future programs that may be of interest to you? If so, check yes, and include your name, email below:

   Yes: ____

   Name: _____ Email: _____

Planning for Any Refreshments

If you are doing your talk for an organization, you generally don't have to bring refreshments, unless the organization asks those doing presentations to bring them. If refreshments are up to you, it's a good idea to provide them, especially for the short arrival and networking period before your presentation. Having refreshments encourages attendees to mix and mingle for about 15 to 30 minutes before you start the regular program.

Preferably keep any refreshments simple, especially for your first program if you expect a small group. You can quickly pick up a beverage and snacks in a few minutes at your local supermarket. For example, at the first Success Secrets program, we provided a few plates of cookies from a nearby Safeway. I also planned to bring a gallon jug of iced tea and cups, though in the rush to get everything together, I left the tea in the fridge at home. That's why it's a good idea to have a checklist of everything you need. As it turned out, none of the few attendees missed the tea, though it would have been nice to have.

Some possibilities for refreshments include the following:

Beverages
- hot coffee or tea in a carton with a pouring spout
- small bottles or cans of water, soda, or juice
- 64 oz. bottles of soda or juice
- A package of 6 oz. or 8 oz. cups

Snacks
- cookies
- nuts
- cupcakes (small bite-sized cupcakes or larger cupcakes cut in half)
- crackers, chips or popcorn
- packaged dips

Include a pile of napkins and small paper plates, if people might do more than grab a single cookie or cracker. For a larger group, you might get platters with veggies, such as carrots and celery, and dips from the supermarket. For a small group, keep it simple.

Allowing Some Time for Networking

Allow some time before the program starts for arrivals and networking. At the end, allow additional time for networking and possibly signing up for other programs, obtaining information on your products and services, and buying any of your products.

With a small group, figure on about 15 to 20 minutes for the check-in and networking; with a larger group, allow 20 to 30 minutes. After the presentation, allow about the same amount of time -- 15 to 20 minutes for a small group; 20 to 30 minutes for a larger group.

Creating a Checklist for Everything to Bring

Since there are so many things to think about in putting on even a small introductory program, it helps to have a checklist. This way you can list everything you are going to bring. If anyone is helping you, indicate on this checklist who is doing what. Organizing your program in this way can help to assure that you have everything you need. You can also use this checklist as a guide for what you need to write, print out, or purchase before the event, so you have everything ready to take to the event.

While I didn't have a checklist and laid out everything I planned to take the night before or in the early afternoon the day of the program, after the fact I wished I had one. That's because I kept thinking about all the things I would need for two days, and every so often I would think "I additionally need to get that." As a result, two hours before the event, I had to scramble to write and print out a few flyers and sign-up forms, and I forgot to bring the beverage for the refreshments. Everything would have gone much more smoothly if I had a checklist.

You can use the following Checklist Form to write in the items you need. If you need more space, add additional rows. You can create additional categories if you have other things to bring.

Checklist of Items for Presentation			
Items to Bring	Where and When to Obtain	Who Is Bringing This	Check If Obtained
Equipment Needed			
Materials for Presentation			
Items to Display			
Promotional Materials			
Sign-Up Table Material			
Handouts and Evaluation Forms			
Refreshments			

CHAPTER 3: MAKING THE ARRANGEMENTS FOR YOUR TALK

If you are doing a talk for an organization, you may not need to do much promotion, since the organization may do much of that for you. You just need to show up and present your program.

Even so, you might help the organization get more attendees if this is a public meeting. It's to your benefit to help with promotion to attract a larger crowd, since the larger the attendance, the more this will help you get future gigs and more attendance in the future.

Alternatively, if you are organizing the event, you need to reach out to your network and the general public interested in your topic to attract attendees. This chapter will discuss promoting both types of events.

Helping an Organization Set Up and Promote an Event

You generally don't have to do anything to help an organization promote your program under these circumstances:
- The program is for members only
- The program is for the employees, managers, or officers of the organization
- The person putting on the program tells you not to do anything, since the organization is taking care of the outreach.

Yet, even if you aren't involved in the promotion, you can still gather the organization's marketing and promotional materials to use in your portfolio of accomplishments. Then, you can use that portfolio to promote your programs to prospective attendees or other organizations that might hire you.

Getting Started in Setting Up Your Own Event

If you are organizing your own event, you have to make a number of arrangements, beginning with determining the date, location, and cost of the event. In turn, the location you can get affects the available dates, and the cost of the location affects how you price the event.

Preferably, start small to keep your costs down, while you are refining your program and building your reputation. As Patrick Schwerdtfeger, a motivational speaker, explained at a workshop I attended: "There's a free circuit, a cheap circuit, and a professional high-priced circuit." Thus, initially, you might start by offering free events that you organize or put on for organizations, and keep the costs low, say by using your home or a free room in a library or bank.

Otherwise, set a low price for the first events you put on, taking into consideration the cost of the venue, refreshments, and your promotional costs to attract attendees. You might also have to figure in the cost of an assistant to help with your promotion, event set-up, or assisting at the sign-in table.

Initially, don't factor in your own time in setting up or conducting the event, since you are still learning to be a professional speaker. But later, as you get more gigs, consider the cost of putting on the event plus your hourly rate for doing other work, and charge accordingly. For example, after your first few events, figure that you should net about $500 to $1500 for each program. But for now, consider that amount a future goal, since your focus should be on developing a good program that others want to attend and building your reputation to attract attendees or get organizations to hire you to put on your program.

Deciding What to Charge Attendees

In deciding what to charge, apart from cost considerations, take into consideration the going rate for speaking programs in your area. If you are in a big city, such as San Francisco or New York, the rate will generally be higher -- say $25-35 for an introductory program, whereas in the surrounding suburbs, the rate will be less -- perhaps $10-15 for a program.

When I was first setting up the cost for my introductory Success Secrets program, my mentor Barbara kept telling me: "You should charge at least $25; you're worth it." But I felt this amount was too much for my first program; I felt more comfortable charging $10 to $15. We compromised at $15 for advance sign-ups until a week before the event, and thereafter $20 to register online or pay $20 at the door. Later, I got confirmation for this pricing from adirector at a local Chamber of Commerce membership director. "$15 for a talk sounds about right," she said.

Deciding on the Date

In choosing a date, consider the dates available for possible venues. A good approach is to have a general idea of the date when you want to hold the event, but be flexible about changing this if the venue you hope to use can't offer you the date you want. Alternatively, choose another venue.

In choosing a date, keep in mind the preferable times to hold your event, based on when your targeted audience is likely to attend. For instance, if you are aiming for professional and business participants, early evenings during the week between about

6:30-9 p.m. are best, and a two hour event is ideal from 6:30-8:30 or 7-10. This way, you allow about 15-30 minutes for arrivals and networking before and about 15-30 minutes after the program, which usually lasts about 60 to 90 minutes.

The best evenings are during the week from Tuesday to Thursday, since Monday is often a stay-at-home evening and sometimes people are just back from a long weekend. It's best to avoid Friday nights, since many people think of this as a date or party night, and it's the beginning of the weekend. Avoid setting up your program on holidays or during the Thanksgiving-Christmas season, because many people will have other plans.

Once you set the date, allow three to four weeks to market and promote the program. For example, after I scheduled my first program for Tuesday evening, October 1st from 6:30 to 8:30, I began promoting it right after Labor Day on Tuesday, September 3rd, giving me a four week window for marketing and PR.

If you are planning a series of programs, set up some tentative dates for scheduling the next events. A good time frame might be once a month if your first event is successful. However, keep these dates tentative in case you decide to postpone or cancel any future programs. You might want to do so if you want to retool your program or decide to seek gigs with organizations rather than planning your own events.

That's what I did. I set up a tentative schedule for two future events on the first Tuesday of November and December, and I created flyers announcing these events with the date and location to be announced. But after I got a relatively small turnout and attended several small business events in the area that also had low turnouts, I decided not to set up my own future events. Instead, I planned to use the video I had made at the event to pitch the program to organizations and corporations. As a result, I told the library where I held my first presentation to release the future dates they were holding for me at no charge. The library's rental coordinator had agreed to this arrangement, so I could decide what to do after assessing the results of my first event.

Deciding on the Location

Once you have a general idea of the date, decide on a venue. A first consideration is the town or city where you want to be. Then, consider the neighborhood where you want to hold the event. Generally, a downtown location is ideal, especially if it is easy to park there or to get there by bus or commuter train.

Additionally, consider the type of venue and the cost. A few tables in a coffee shop or bar can be fine for a free introductory event. But if you're charging, you want a separate room, which you can set up with tables, chairs, and possibly projection equipment for a PowerPoint or video. Also. select a venue that will be quiet for a presentation, so a private room in a restaurant or bar may not work well, if there is noise from the main room. So ask about the ambience in the room when you consider potential venues.

Take into consideration the likely size of your group. If possible, look for a place where you might have some flexibility, in case you get more or less people than expected.

Unless you expect your talk to attract a large following, start small with a room for 10 to 20 people, since your cost for a smaller room will generally be less. Should the event draw a bigger audience than expected, the location you have chosen may have a larger room available; if not, you can find a larger venue and forgo your initial deposit, since the fees paid by a larger attendance will generally cover this cost.

Once you find a suitable venue, if possible, arrange to tentatively hold the space for the next one or two dates you are planning. Then, if your first event goes well, you already have the next locations lined up. But preferably, don't make a financial commitment until you see how the first event goes, because if you don't get the expected turnout, you can easily cancel the dates. This flexible approach makes a lot of sense if you decide to change your focus after the first event from organizing your own events to using your experience -- and a video if you create one -- to help you get future gigs from other organizations which will handle the arrangements for you. Later, you can always shift back to organizing your own events after you do events for different organizations and build a following.

Some potential venues are rooms in the following:
- library
- bank
- club house
- hotel
- motel complex
- country clubs

If you have been to events in these venues, you can assess whether they would be suitable for your program. You can also get referrals from others in your business and personal networks. Or try looking for venues by a search on Google. Just put in the type of venue you are looking for and the name of the city where you want to hold the event. Then, call to find out if the venue has rooms for meetings. As to speak to the person in charge of room rentals and reservations.

In my case, I started out by first going to an art gallery and meeting space that my mentor Barbara recommended. The owner had just started renting out the space and was already having successful events with an upscale crowd that might be interested in my event. However, when I met the owner and her business adviser, they pulled out a contract requiring half down to book the date, and I discovered that the cost would be $500, or if I wanted to commit to three dates, $450 each. The owner suggested that I could readily get that money back if I had 20 attendees at $25 each. But I wasn't sure I could get that many people to my first event. I also felt that $25 was too much to charge attendees for a short introductory program, since I was relatively unknown as a speaker. So I graciously declined.

Then, fortunately, I found the venue I booked fairly quickly, since I had been to events at the local library, which had several different rooms available at a much lower cost. The prices ranged from $60 to $105 for private parties and business groups to $40 to $80 for non-profit groups. Even better, since I was just starting out, the rental coordinator agreed to give me the non-profit rate. So in the hopes of a large turnout of 35 to 40 people, I chose a bigger room for two hours at $80 an hour rather than a smaller room seating up to 20 people for $40 an hour. Perhaps in the end, it was a good arrangement, since there was plenty of space for the videographer to film the presentation and a display of books on two tables. But the room was certainly too large and more expensive than necessary for the half-dozen people who showed up.

Thus, think realistically about the likely turnout for your event and plan on your space accordingly. Initially, keep it small, though be ready to go larger if you attract a larger crowd than expected.

Determining the Costs for the Space You Rent

When you consider different venues and costs, it can be simple to choose a room, if the venue has a single type of room and rate which can vary depending on the time and day of the week. Commonly, the day rate from 8 a.m. to 5 p.m. will be less, while the rate for weekday evenings from 5 p.m. to 11 p.m. may be higher, and the highest rate may be for Friday evening and weekend bookings.

However, if the venue has multiple rooms and times, once you determine the time and date, decide which room would be most suitable based on the size of group you expect.

In addition, some venues will offer other services for additional fees. For instance, the library venue I chose additionally offered audiovisual and other staff assistance, a weekly e-newsletter with event advertisements, a kitchen usage fee in its larger room, and a video recording fee. I could even rent table linens to cover the tables.

To illustrate, here are the options offered by the Lafayette Library where I held my first event. Likewise, you may get a similar sheet with costs for different rooms and times from venues with multiple options.

LAFAYETTE LIBRARY and LEARNING CENTER FOUNDATION

ROOM RENTAL RATES

	Don Tatzin Community Hall or Amphitheater	Arts & Science Discovery Center	Oak Conference Room
	2-3 hour minimum	2-3 hour minimum	
Private Party/Business Rates	hourly rate	hourly rate	hourly rate
Monday - Sunday 8 am - 5 pm	$120	$90	$60
Monday - Thursday 5 pm - 11 pm	$135	$105	$60 ('til 10pm)
Friday - Sunday 5 pm - 11 pm (3 hr. min.)	$210	$155	n/a
Non-Profit 501(c)(3) & Tenant Rates	hourly rate	hourly rate	hourly rate
Monday - Sunday 8 am - 5 pm	$95	$65	$40
Monday - Thursday 5 pm - 11 pm	$110	$80	$40 (until 10pm)
Friday - Sunday 5 pm - 11 pm (3 hr. min.)	$160	$105	n/a
Miscellaneous Fees			
Audiovisual or other Staff Assistance*	$25/hour		
Weekly E-Newsletter Event Advertisement	$40/entry		
Kitchen Usage Fee (Community Hall only)	$45		
Piano Fee (Community Hall only)	$75 - $100		
Janitorial Fee (applied to large parties and when extensive wear or damage occurs)	$150		
Refundable Security Deposit (as needed)	$500		
Video Recording Fee	Non-Profit: $100/Private: $125		
Table Linens (Limited Selection)	$10/each		
Use of LLLC Lobby after hours (with Community Hall Rental only)	$100/hour		

To reserve, contact (925) 283-6513 ext. 103 or rentals@LLLCF.org

*Use of facility or planning/consulting services beyond the included 30 minute allotment is subject to additional charge.

All credit card payments will be subject to a transaction processing fee. Thank you for your understanding.

Revised January 2019

Booking the Venue for Your Event

Once you are deciding on a venue for your event, consider the rental policies, which can affect your decision to book the venue. For instance, if you want to sell anything or collect money at the door, be sure you can do this. The organization may also have other policies you have to agree to and require you to assume certain responsibilities. These responsibilities might include taking care of any set up and clean up after the event during the time you have booked. You may also be financially liable for any damages to the property or injuries to attendees at the event unless you or your venue have insurance that covers this

For example, here are some typical rental policies:
- Your event can't interfere with other activities at the location.
- You will confine the activities of your event to the space rented and to the restrooms.

- You shall allow for set up and clean up time during your rental period, although some organizations may allow you an extra 15 minutes for set-up and clean up.
- You may have to submit any of your materials to publicize the event to the organization, and if there are multiple rooms at that location, you have to specify which room you are renting.
- You can't use certain types of materials to put up decorations on the walls, such as nails, tacks, staples, or sticky tape.
- You can't put up permanent signs on or adjacent to the building, though you can put up temporary portable signs.
- You can't discriminate in your event due to race, religion, color, national origin, ancestry, gender, disability, age, or sexual orientation.
- You have to put a deposit of the estimated total balance and then have to pay the remaining balance within a week after or at least a week before your rental.
- Under certain circumstances, you may need to have a certificate of insurance, although this isn't usual for small speaking engagements.
- You are responsible to set up and remove all decorations and outside equipment, and you have to clear off tables and chairs, put any trash away, and clean up any spills or stains.
- You have to remove any property you bring in to the event.
- You have to assume the sole responsibility for any accidents or injuries to persons or property resulting from your use of the venue.
- You are responsible for the control and supervision of anyone attending the event, including making sure that the venue suffers no damage and that everyone conducts themselves in an orderly manner.
- If you plan to sell alcoholic beverages, you need to obtain a license in advance to do so.

Such policies may seem daunting when you just want to put on a simple speaking event, particularly if you only expect a small number of attendees at your first event. But these policies are for everyone's protection, and you are likely to do all of the things required anyway in putting on the event. In my case, I reviewed the list of policies very quickly, put them aside, and none of these issues came up before, during, or after the event.

Here's the library policy statement I received, as an example of the type of policy statement you might expect to get from a venue.

Lafayette Library and Learning Center Foundation
Rentals@LLLCF.org ✦ (925) 283-6513 x103 ✦ 3491 Mt. Diablo Blvd, Suite 214 Lafayette, CA 94549

LLLCF Rental Policies
www.lllcf.org/rental-policies

Rental Policies and General Information
- All fees and use regulations are subject to change.
- Rental Agreements cannot be transferred, assigned, sublet or issued to minors.
- Use of the facilities cannot interfere with regular County Library operations and programs.
- Renter shall restrict all activities to the area(s) so designated and to the restrooms.
- Set up and clean up time must be accounted for in your rental time.
- Storage (for food/beverages, decorations, equipment, rentals, etc.) is not available either before or after an event.
- LLLCF has the right to review materials used to publicize events held at LLLC as well as proposed entertainment. Please ensure to specify the name of the room/space that you are renting on your event publicity (i.e. "The Oak Conference Room at the LLLC").
- All decorations must be approved and flame retardant. Use of nails, tacks, staples, sticky tape, confetti, uncontained candles, aerosol streamers, sand, hay, etc. are prohibited.
- For large parties or events, as determined by LLLCF, a $150 janitorial fee will be charged.
- Applicant shall exhibit no permanent signs on or adjacent to the building. Temporary portable signs may be exhibited during rental period with prior authorization.
- We do not rent to any individual or group that discriminates because of race, religion, color, national origin, ancestry, gender, disability, age or sexual orientation.

Deposits, Payments, and Cancellations
- Your rental is not confirmed until LLLCF has received a signed Rental Agreement and a deposit of 50% of the estimated total balance. The remaining balance is due one week after your rental.
- **Cancellations must be made in writing and any deposit paid will be forfeited.**
- Cancellations made less than 14 days in advance may be subject to loss of the entire rental fee.
- The LLLCF reserves the right to reschedule, relocate or deny a request of a previously confirmed reservation.

Security Deposits, Damages, and Insurance
- A $500 security deposit may be required for large parties and sit-down meals and if required, will be billed in advance and is due no later than 30 days before the event. Charges for extra cleaning, damage to the facility, furnishings and/or property, and overtime fees will result in a deduction or forfeit of deposit. Renters will be billed for damages not covered by the deposit. If property is not vacated by end of the contractual period, associated costs will be deducted from security deposit or billed accordingly.
- When a certificate of insurance is required, obtain this from your insurance company naming the City of Lafayette, the Lafayette Library and Learning Center Foundation, and the Lafayette Library and Learning Center and its employees and agents as additional insured and indicating that your insurance coverage is primary. The amount of the insurance should be for no less than $1 million.

Responsibilities
- Renters are responsible for set-up and removal of all decorations and outside equipment. Tables/chairs are to be cleared off and trash placed in appropriate receptacles. Spills/stains are to be cleaned from floors. Kitchen area is to be cleaned and all personal items removed.
- All property brought in by renters must be removed at end of the rental. We cannot guarantee the return of any items left behind.
- Renters are solely responsible and answerable financially for any and all accidents or injuries to persons or property resulting from the use of Library facilities.
- Renters shall be responsible for the control and supervision of all people in attendance during the usage of the facility and shall take care to see that the facility suffers no damage, and that everyone conducts him/herself in an orderly manner. If damages or behavior of the group warrant, a function may be stopped in progress, and renter may be denied further use of the facilities.

Alcoholic Beverage Policy

If alcoholic beverages will be sold, a license must be obtained in advance from the Alcoholic Beverage Control Board. This includes direct exchange of money for beverages, purchase of tickets that may be exchanged for beverages, or purchase of a dinner or event ticket that includes the service of alcoholic beverages. For more information and to download Form 221, go to www.abc.ca.gov.

Please retain this copy for your records.

Finally, when you book the venue, you will normally be asked to fill in and sign a rental agreement. This agreement will include the event date, your contact information, and your type of organization or company, such as if you are a private organization or a non-profit. You will also be asked to indicate the arrival time, start and end time of the event, and the time you intend to leave.

Some other questions may be about the type of event, such as if it's open to the public, if it's free, if you are serving a meal or refreshments, if you plan to have alcoholic beverages, and the number of attendees expected.

Other questions may deal with the room set-up, since the venue organizer may set up the room before you arrive. For instance, the organizer may ask: Do you prefer theater, classroom, or boardroom style seating? How many tables would you like and how would you like them arranged? Would you like a registration or welcome table in the room, and if so where? Do you want to a podium, screen, or projector? Can you use an easel or table linens?

If additional services are available, such as audiovisual or staff assistance or advertising your event in the venue's newsletter, the venue organizer will ask if you are interested in that.

Here's an example of the agreement I filled out after I decided to use the Arts & Science Discovery Center at the Lafayette Library.

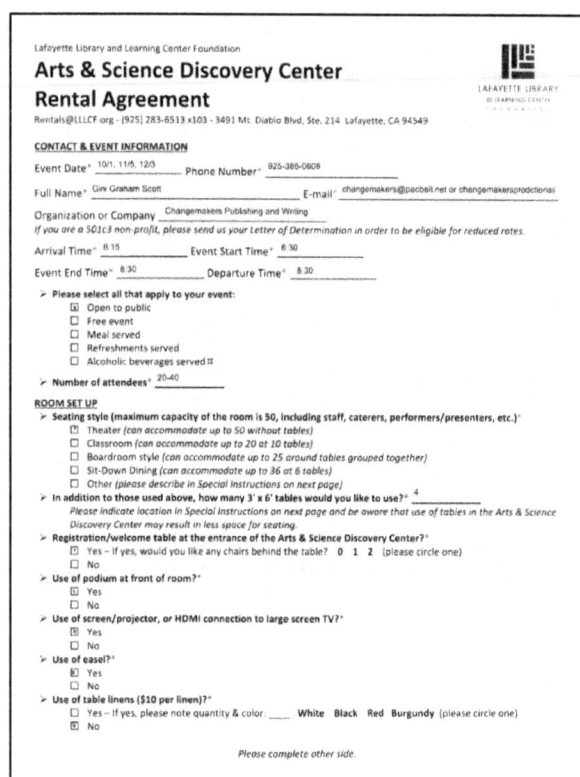
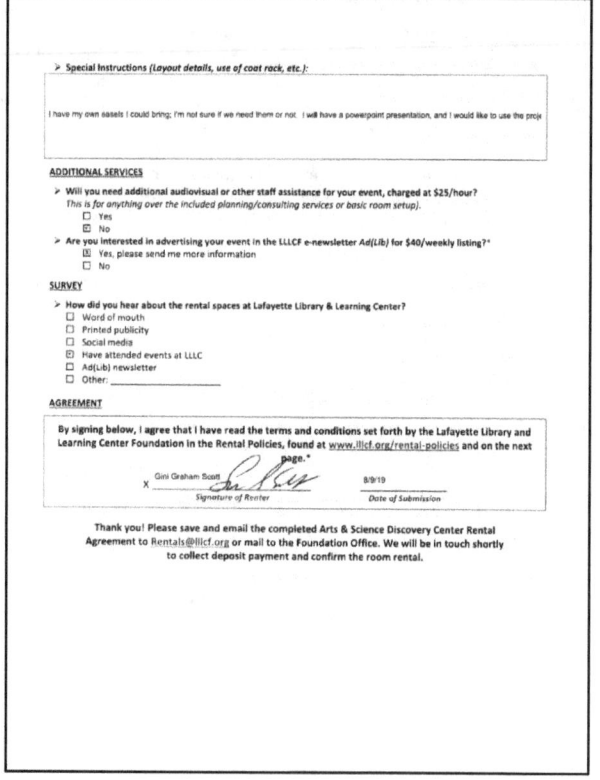

CHAPTER 4: MARKETING AND PROMOTING YOUR TALK

Promoting Your Event for an Organization

Although you may not need to do anything to set up or promote an event if you are only appearing as a speaker, find out how many people to expect and if you can sell at the event, so you can plan accordingly. For instance, by knowing the expected audience, you can decide what kind of sales and promotional material to bring, as well as how many items you hope to sell. This information will also help you determine how many flyers or other materials to bring to promote future events. Whether you bring promotional materials or not, bring business cards and a sign-up form, so you can notify attendees about your future programs and items for sale.

If you can help the organization promote the event, do so, and find out how you can help. Often any promotional efforts will be much like what you might do to promote an event you organize yourself, though you might more actively promote your own event. Some of the things you might do include:
-passing out flyers at business referral and networking groups,
-announcing the event on your social media groups, like Facebook and Instagram
-providing announcements about the event to organizations you belong to so they can include in their newsletter
-inviting friends and associates to attend the event

If this is a paid event, you might sometimes be able to offer your friends or associates a guest pass or discount, so ask about that. The guest pass or discount might give those you invite an incentive to come, and your invitees will appreciate the offer.

Places to Market and Promote Your Event

If this is your own event, think of the different ways you can reach your target audience. One approach is to set up your event on services where attendees need to sign up and pay in advance. Then, you can direct your promotion to get prospective attendees to RSVP there, although they might still be able to pay in other ways, such as through PayPal, a credit card, or at the door.

It's a good idea to offer a variety of options to R.S.V.P. and pay to encourage more attendees. Later, you can decide what works best and use those promotional approaches in the future.

Setting Up Your Event on Event and Meeting Platforms

The advantage of using one of the event or meeting platforms is they take care of the booking details. If you are putting on a paid event, these platforms handle the payments for you in return for a service fee paid by you or the participant. In some cases, you will get paid after your event concludes successfully; in other cases, individuals pay up front but get a refund if you cancel the event.

Two of the most popular services which I used are Eventbrite and Meetup. I'll describe how to set up your own event using these services.

Creating an Event on Eventbrite

Eventbrite makes it very easy to set up an event, and it provides guidelines you can follow. To illustrate, here's how I set up my Success Secrets event.

First, you need to set up an account, which includes entering basic information about yourself, your company name if any, and your address, email, and bank routing number and account, in order to pay you after the event. Once your Eventbrite account is set up, your sign-in page will look something like this.

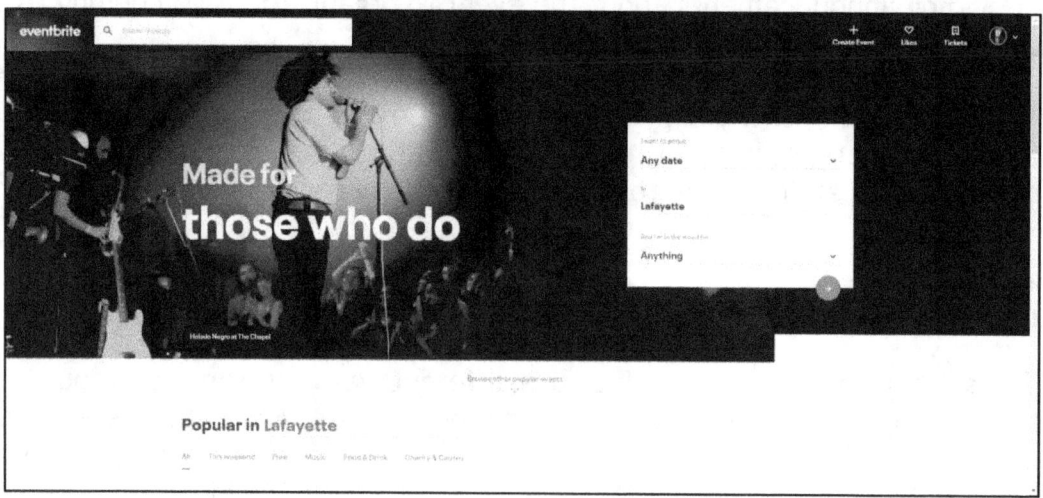

After you set-up your account, you create your event by clicking the "Create An Event" button. It is helpful to prepare the copy for your event in advance, so you can readily copy and paste it into the event description, rather than trying to create it on the spot. In writing your description, think of it as marketing copy in which you quickly describe what the event is about and the value the attendee will get by attending. You can streamline the process by developing some basic marketing copy you use on different platforms for marketing your event

To start creating the event, enter in the Event Title, Location, and the Date and Time when the event starts and ends.

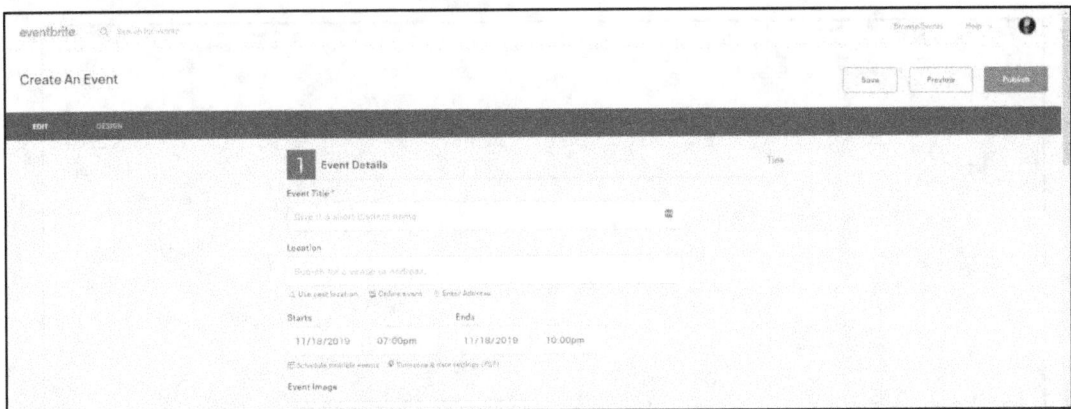

Also include an image of the event. This can be one of your photos, such as of a meeting you previously conducted or a photo on the subject of your talk. Or you can get a stock photo, or combine your own photo with a stock photo, which is what I did.

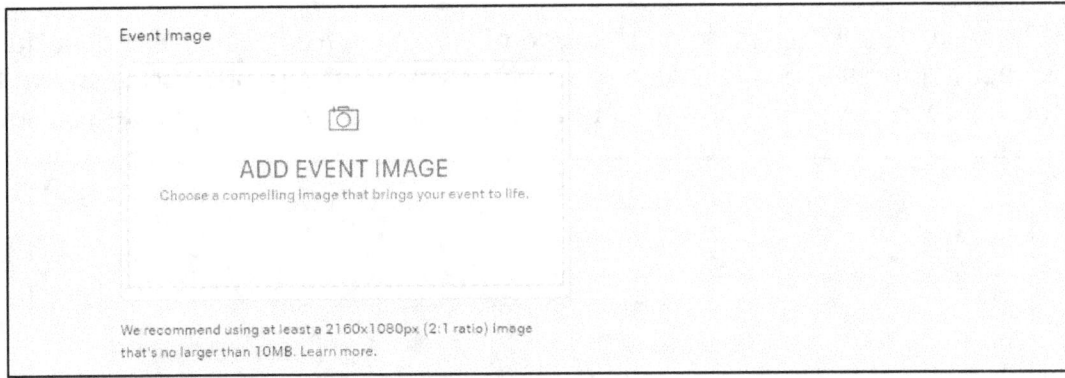

As illustrated below, I combined a photo of myself with a stock photo of an audience at an event being filmed by a videographer.

Then, add the event description, followed by the name and description of the organizer. If you are on Facebook or Twitter, you can link your event listing there.

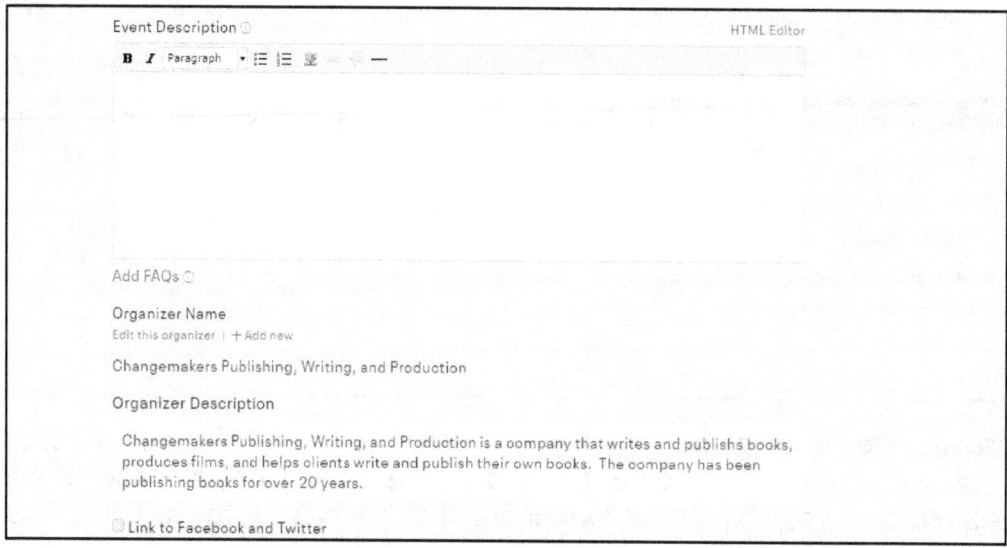

The next step is to decide on the type of tickets -- free, paid, or a donation. Then, select additional settings, such as whether you want a public listing shown to everyone (of course, you do) or a private listing, shown only to the people you specify.

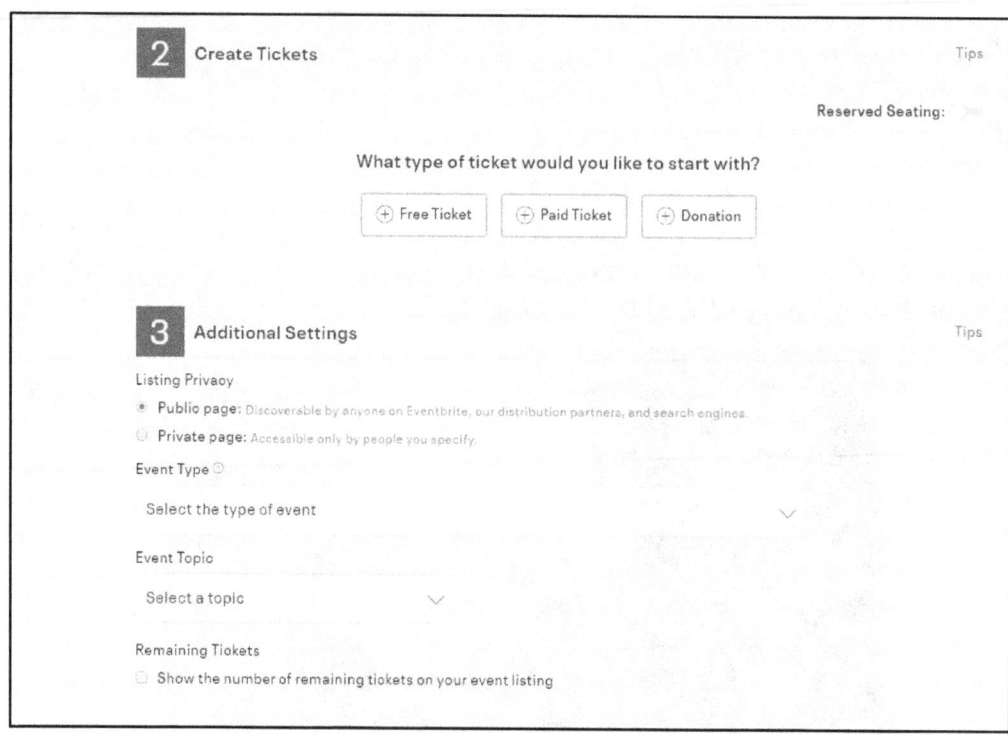

You can additionally indicate the type of event and event topic.

Select the type of event	
Appearance or Signing	Auto, Boat & Air
Attraction	Business & Professional
Camp, Trip, or Retreat	Charity & Causes
Class, Training, or Workshop	Community & Culture
Concert or Performance	Family & Education
Conference	Fashion & Beauty
Convention	Film, Media & Entertainment
Dinner or Gala	Food & Drink
Festival or Fair	Government & Politics
Game or Competition	Health & Wellness
Meeting or Networking Event	Hobbies & Special Interest
Other	Home & Lifestyle
Party or Social Gathering	Music
Race or Endurance Event	Other
Rally	Performing & Visual Arts
Screening	Religion & Spirituality
Seminar or Talk	School Activities
Tour	Science & Technology
Tournament	Seasonal & Holiday
	Sports & Fitness
	Select a topic

While you have an option of showing the number of tickets remaining, it might be better not to include this, unless you expect a lot of early sign-ups, because prospective attendees might be discouraged from signing up, if you have a large number of tickets remaining for the event.

Once you enter all of this information, you can save it as a draft. When you are ready, make your event live.

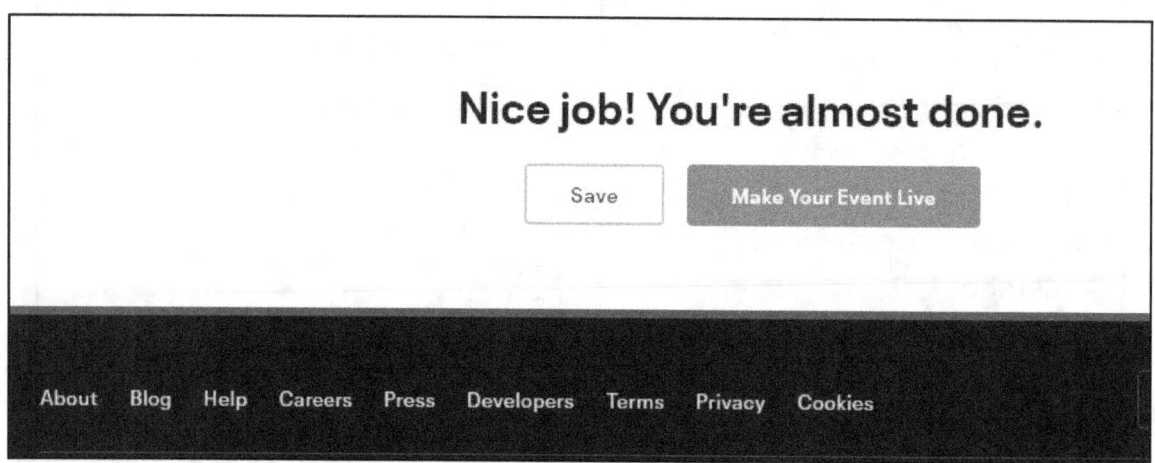

As an example, here's what my event looked like with the initial information followed by the event description, and a few tags at the end that further categorized the event.

Here's the opening header for the announcement.

Here's an example of my description, followed by a brief bio and the tags.

Description

SUCCESS SECRETS IN EVERYDAY LIFE

with Gini Graham Scott

Author of 200+ Books from Self-Help and Business to Novels and Kids Books
Writer/Executive Producer of 10 Films

You're invited to a special introduction to a woman with amazing career and how to apply her success secrets in your everyday life. Find new ways to tap into your creativity and enhance your life and work.

This event features a special introduction of Gini Graham Scott, interviewed by Barbara Edwards, a Business Coach, and former CEO of California Hosts. They'll be talking about how you can apply Gini's success secrets in your everyday life. Gini has published over 200 books from self-help and business books to novels and kids' books. She is also the writer/executive producer of 10 feature films, documentaries, and TV series, and a Lafayette resident for 5 years.

Barbara Edwards will interview Gini about how she achieved her incredible career, based on not only writing and publishing books and producing films, but designing over two dozen published games, 100+ songs, and several dozen music videos.

For the first time, see trailers for Gini's 6 latest films. Two feature over 30 Contra Costa Residents: *Me, My Dog, and I* and *The New Age of Aging*

Gini will also share her secret tips on how she was able to achieve so much and how you can do it, too, whatever your goals, hopes, and dreams. You can ask plenty of questions about her suggestions for you.

Date And Time

Tue, October 1, 2019
6:30 PM – 8:30 PM PDT
Add to Calendar

Location

Lafayette Library
Art & Discovery Room
3491 Mt. Diablo Blvd.
Lafayette, California 94549
View Map

Refund Policy

No Refunds

Here's a brief bio:

Gini Graham Scott, Ph.D., CEO of Changemakers Publishing and Writing, an internationally known writer, consultant, speaker, and workshop leader. Her recent books include *Increase Your Impact and Influence*, *Self-Publish Your Book in Multiple Formats*, the *New World Neanderthals*, and *The Secret World of the Little Imps*. Her latest films include *The New Age of Aging*, *Me, My Dog, and I*, *Infidelity*, and *Rescue Me*. She has published over 50 books with major publishers and 150+ books through Changemakers Publishing on social trends, business, self-help, and for kids. She has worked with hundreds of clients as a ghostwriter for books and scripts, and as a communications strategist and consultant. Her website is www.changemakerspublishingandwriting.com.

Tags

United States Events | California Events | Things To Do In Lafayette, CA
Lafayette Seminars | Lafayette Business Seminars

To help prospective attendees find where your event will be held and decide if this is a convenient location for them, Eventbrite includes a map with your location,

Since I provided a link to Facebook, here's what my Eventbrite announcement looked like there.

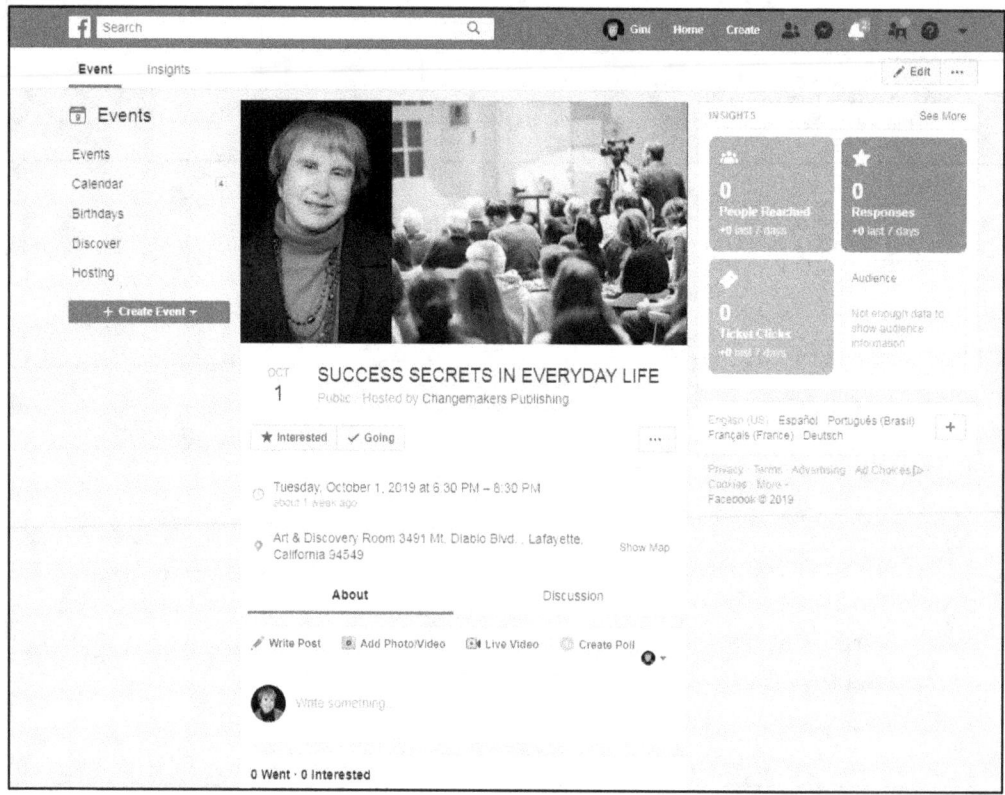

Thus, Eventbrite can be an effective platform for marketing for your event. Once it is set up, you can direct people there in your flyers and in any advertising, promotion, interviews, or however else you get people to come to your event. In fact, I found that all of the attendees who showed up registered on Eventbrite.

Creating an Event on Meetup

Another good platform for getting event sign-ups is creating a Meetup group and posting your event there. If you already have a Meetup group, just add the event.

To initially join Meetup, you have to set up an account. You can opt to pay on a monthly basis or for six months.

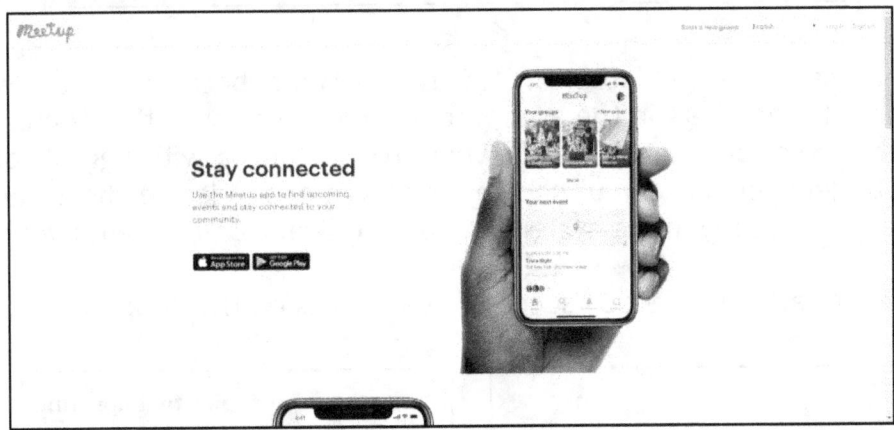

After you click the "Start a New Group" page, you will receive an invitation to "Get Started."

Then, enter the group's location.

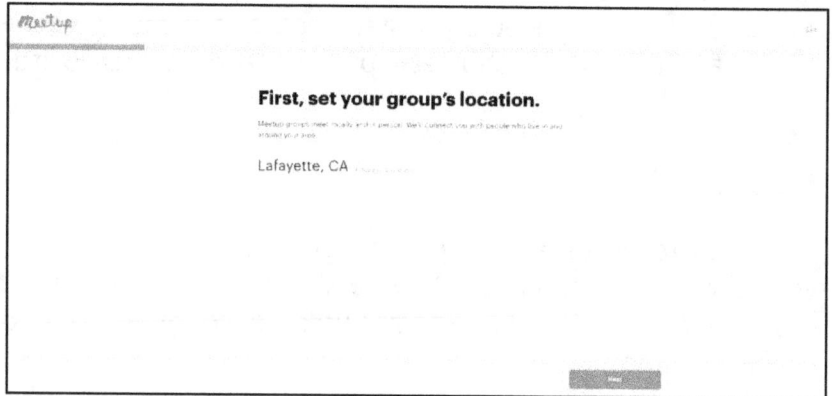

After that, select up to 15 topics. This is important, because Meetup will send an announcement to members in the area who have an interest in that topic.

Select the topics of interest that fit your group. Meetup will suggest some related topics to help you make your choice, and it's a good idea to choose among them since they are already in the system, though you can come up with your own topics, too.

For instance, after I entered "success", the topics on the popped up.

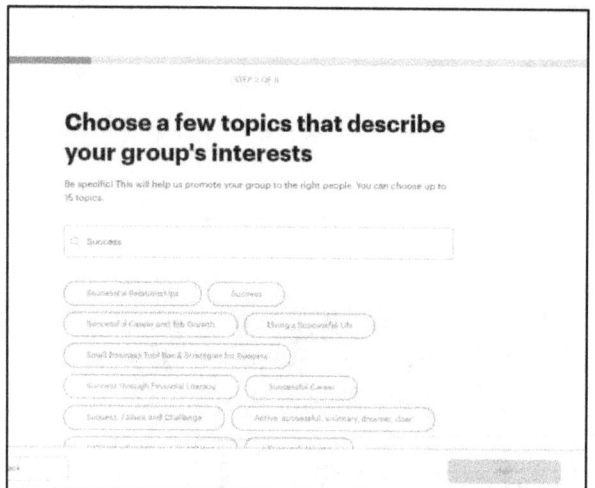 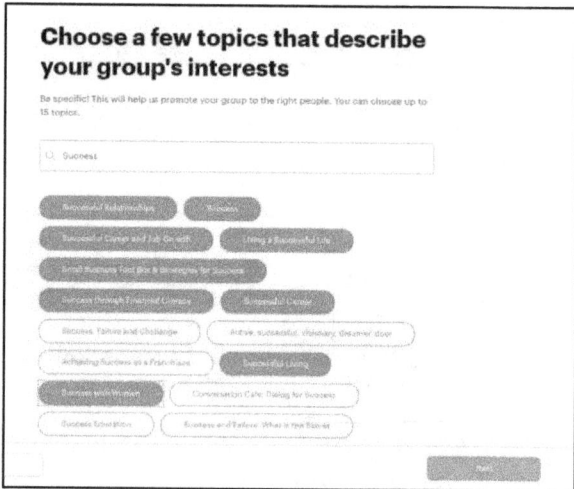

The next step is to pick an appealing name. This could be the name of your event, or choose a more general name to encompass the different topics you plan to include in your speaking program. Meetup will suggest a possible name, based on your location and topics, but you can choose whatever name you want.

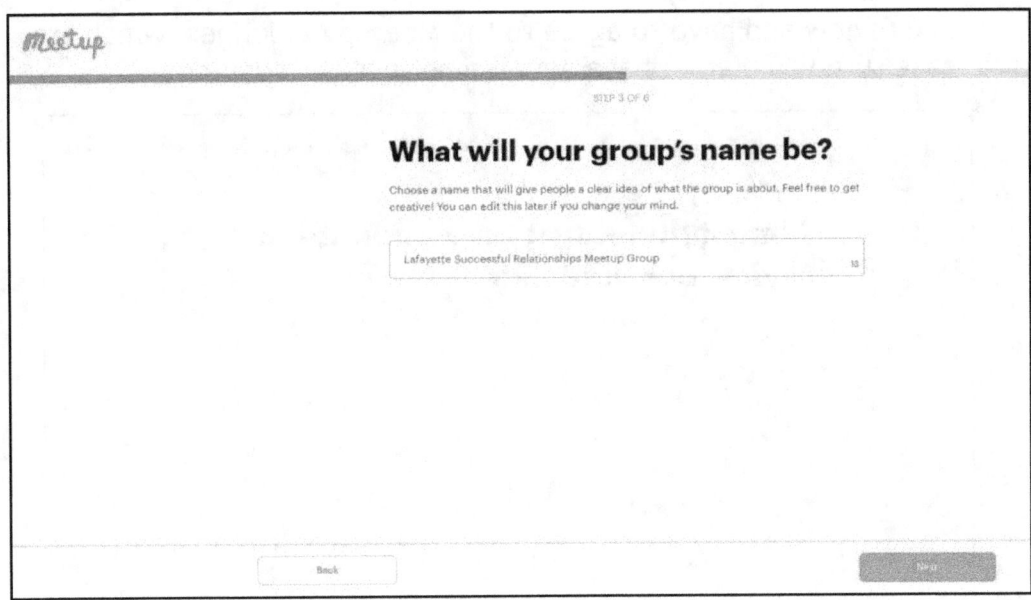

Next, write a brief group description indicating the group's purpose and what it will do. Meetup has a suggestion you can use as a guide.

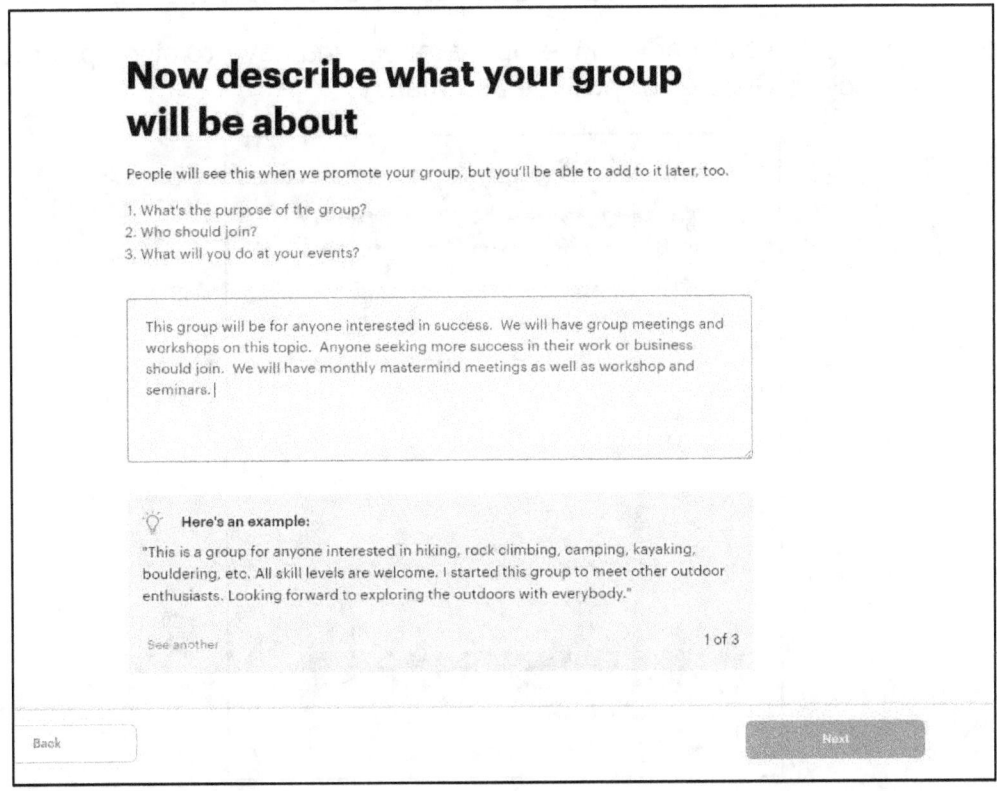

Then, you review and have to agree to the Meetup guidelines, which are designed to make sure you plan to have actual meetings. And you do.

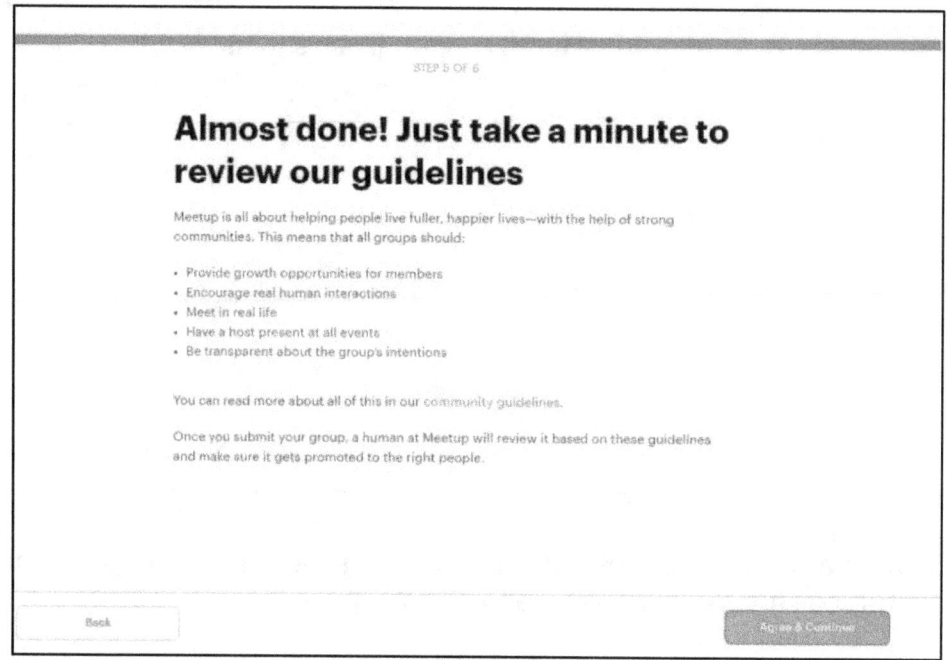

Then, if you are not already a Meetup member, you have to sign up through your account on Facebook or Google, or provide an email.

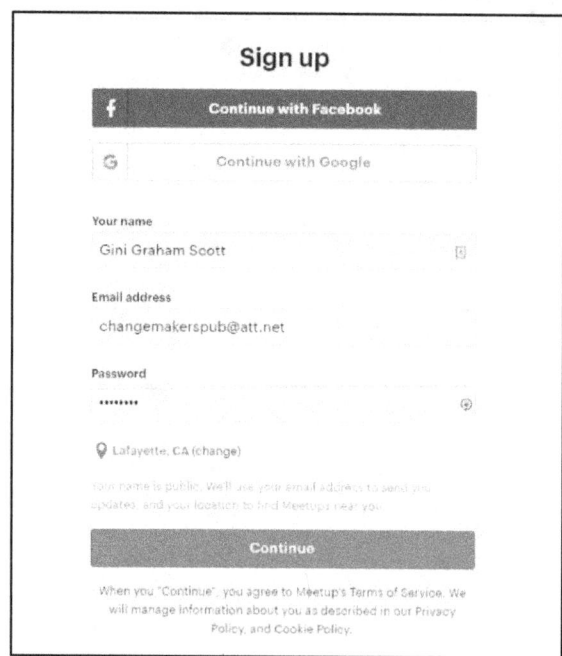

Then, you get an option to pay on a monthly basis or every six months. And as a new subscriber, you get an extra discount.

Payment options
You're just one step away from starting Successful Relationships in Lafayette!

○ Pay monthly
$23.99 $16.79 per month

● Pay every 6 months **BEST VALUE**
$16.49 $11.54 x 6 months

Special discount: 30% off today's order
Your discount has been automatically applied to today's payment.

Payment information

Name on card

Card number

CVC

Expiration date
Month   Year

ZIP / Postal code

Your Meetup subscription includes:
✓ Promotion of your new group to potential members in your area
✓ Quick and easy tools for scheduling events and staying in touch with your members
✓ Access to customer support 7 days a week

    Once you pay, your new group is set up and you can add additional sections to provide more details about the group, yourself, and your event. Preferably, have all of the information about your group and event ready to go. That's because in a day or two, Meetup will send an announcement about your group to everyone in your area interested in your topic. Those who are interested can request to join. They will then be automatically enrolled, unless you indicate that you want to review all interested Meetup members first. Unless you have a special reason for reviewing applications, let anyone who wants to join do so. This way you are more likely to get sign-ups in your group. However, wait a few days until you get members, at least 15 to 20 members, before you announce your event.

    After you pay, you can create your event, using Meetup's guidelines about what to include. If you want to charge money, you can offer various pay options, including PayPal, credit card, or paying at the door. Preferably, set up the payment through Meetups WePay portal, so people have to pay to attend. That way you are more assured they will attend, in that only about 30-50% of the people who sign up without paying generally come. To use the WePay portal, provide your bank account routing code and account number, and as people pay, the money goes directly to your account.

To illustrate how this works, I have included screen shots of my group set-up and the event posting for Success Secrets in Everyday Life. Although Meetup sent me a few messages to say "You haven't announced your meeting yet," I waited about a week until I had about 35 members in the group to send out the announcement.

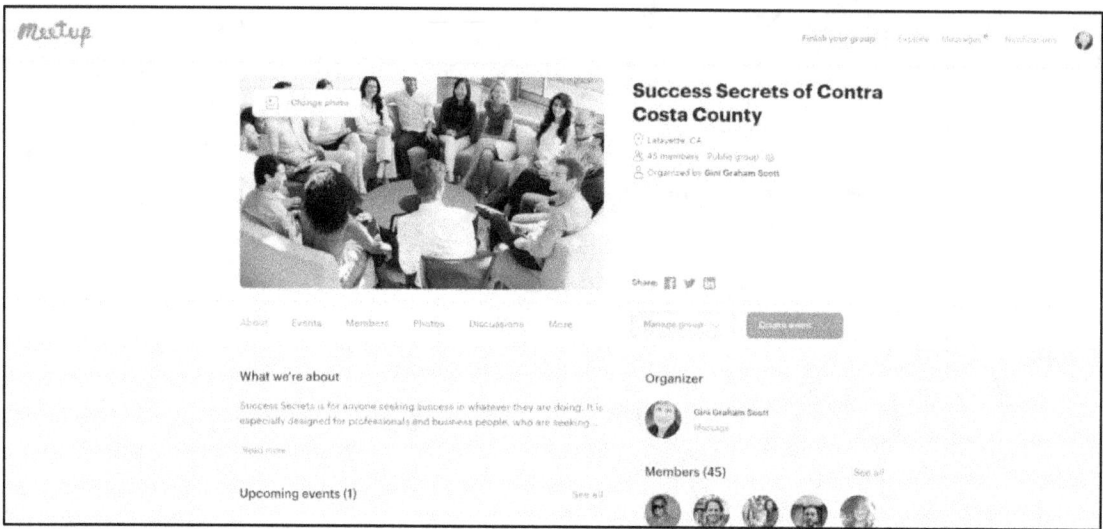

As illustrated, each group starts with its name and location, followed by the number of members and the organizer. Additionally, there is a group description and photo of the organizer. As members join, Meetup adds their picture or logo.

There is also a group photo by the name of the group. For this photo, I chose a stock picture showing people in a meeting. Should people want to read more, they can see the full group description, as indicated below.

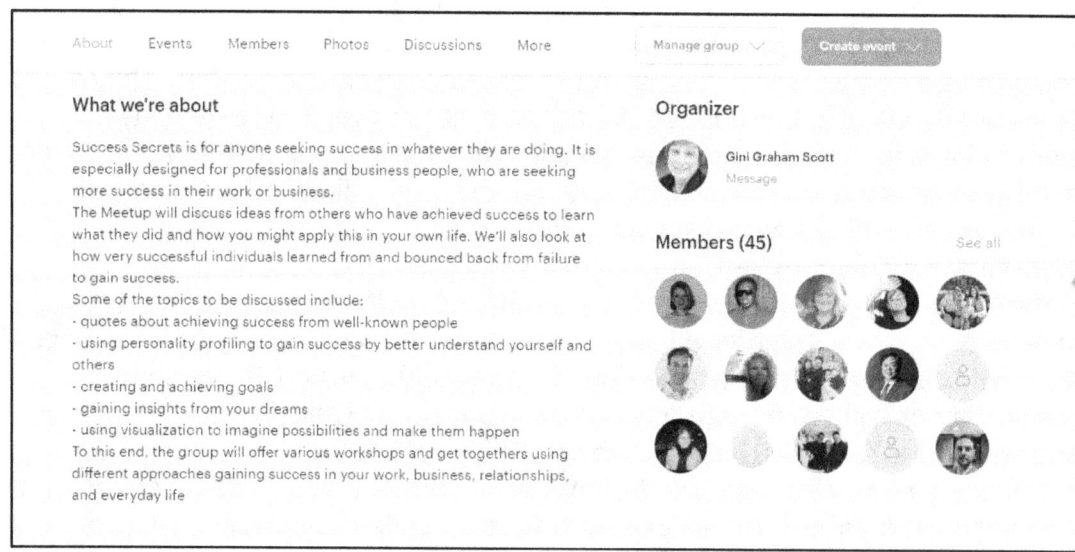

Once you set up your event, it will be listed as an upcoming event and you will be listed as "1 attendee." As others sign up, they will be added to the listing.

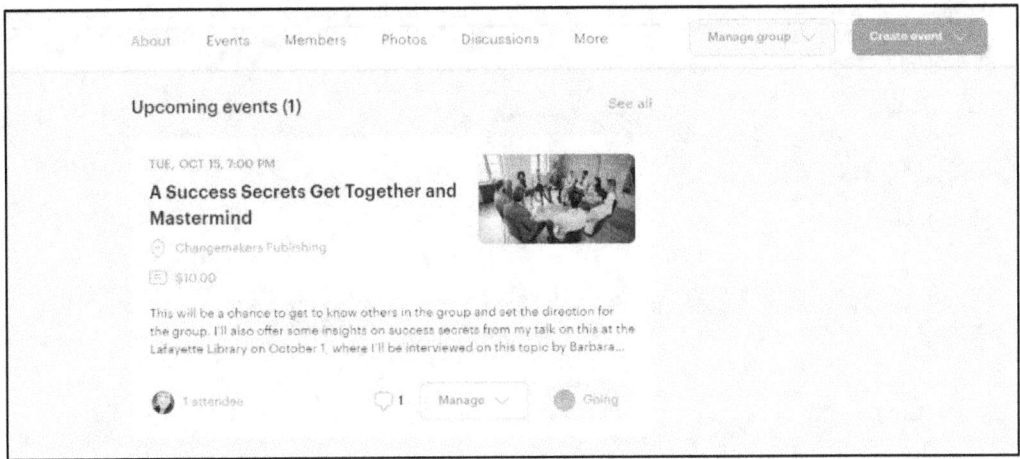

Here's what a final event set up looks like, which includes the name of the event, host, date, time, location address, map, event photo, and details of the event.

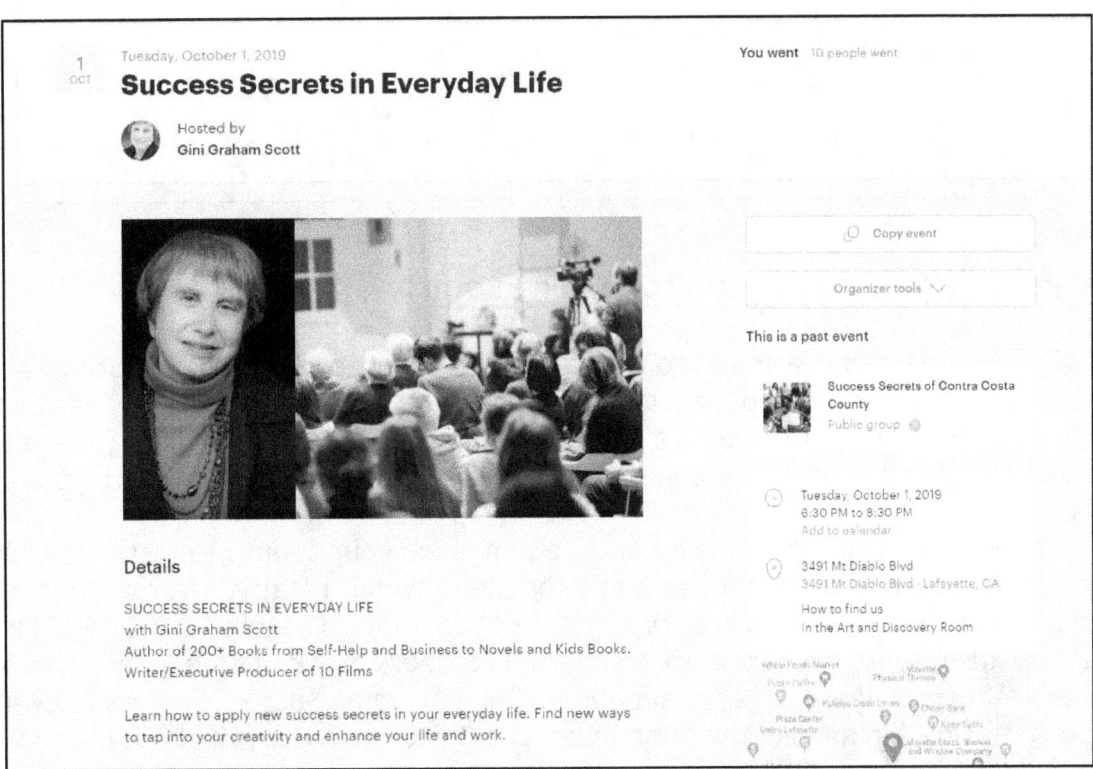

If you have further details, you can add them. In this case, I preferred that people sign up through Eventbrite, so I included that link in the description, although if people could pay through Meetup, I would have indicated that here.

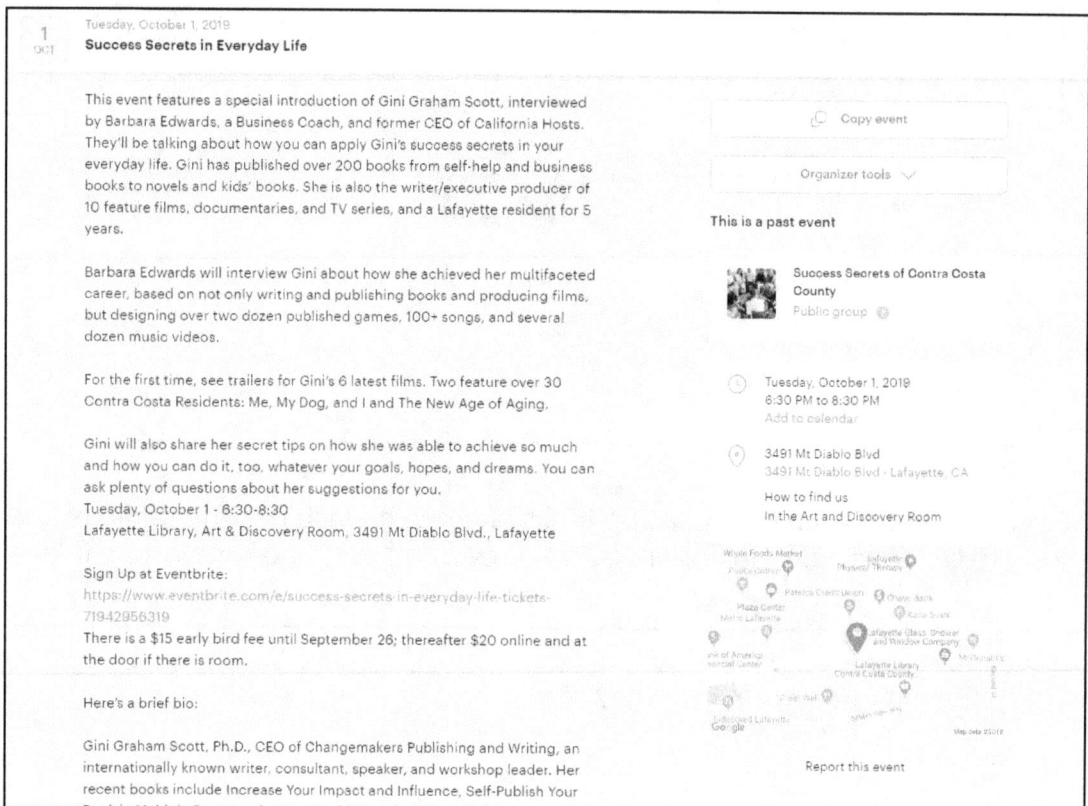

Creating Promotional Flyers for Your Event

Promotional flyers are a good way to promote your event by distributing them at networking and referral group meetings. You can hand them out personally as you talk to different people or put them on a display table. You can also put flyers in retail stores, at your local chamber of commerce, or send them as attachments to your email contacts.

At some meetings you may be able to announce your event or briefly describe your business at a raffle if you offer a gift for the drawing. Ideally, offer a gift that introduces people to your business or event. For example, I regularly offer a book as a gift at the after-hour mixers sponsored by the chambers of commerce where I am a member. At one of these mixers I announced my upcoming Success Secrets in Everyday Life presentation. In making the announcement, I held up a copy of the flyer and invited anyone interested to pick up a flyer to learn more.

In writing your copy on the flyer, keep it short. Emphasize the topic of your talk and how attendees can benefit by attending the program. Include the date and time of the event, location, and address. If you have arranged for sign-ups through Eventbrite or other event sign-up service, include the link to your event, so people can sign up there. Generally, a posting for your event on Meetup doesn't work well for a promotional flyer, because people have to join Meetup to register for your event, and many people who get your flyer may not be on Meetup.

Use a photo or two, and use large type on the top third or half of the flyer. Then, describe the program in about 75 to 100 words. You can use a text box to highlight some special feature, and as relevant, include a short bio about yourself or your company. If you have already written up an event description for a platform like Eventbrite or Meetup, you can draw on that for your flyer, though you may need to shorten the longer description.

For a professional look, you can hire a copywriter or marketing company to create your flyer with full-color photos or graphics. The cost can range from about $50 to $500, depending on the experience of individual or company you hire. If this is your first speaking gig or you are beginning to speak, you want to keep costs low and use this to help get future gigs.

Thus, it's best to start small, and you can easily create a basic flyer in Word and print it on colored paper so it will stand out. Choose a color that reflects your message. For instance, I used a light golden paper for my flyer, since gold suggests wealth and success. Think of the color associations with your service, product, or topic, such as light green for money, light brown for nature, pink for a beauty product or service, and so on.

Another advantage of creating your own flyer in Word or other easy-to-use platform, such as Photoshop or Canva, is you can print a small number to start. Say print 20 to 50 flyers at first, rather than a much longer run for a flyer created by a professional.

This DIY approach gives you more flexibility, so you can test out the response after a short run and make any edits to create a revised copy. If you make any revisions, do another test and compare the results with different versions to see what approach results in the most responses. You might additionally get feedback from friends and associates.

As an example, here's a flyer I used, which features a photo, some headline copy, a link to Eventbrite, a short description, and a brief bio. Though I used a color photo, this was only apparent when I sent the Word document or PDF in response to a request for more information. Otherwise, when I printed the flyers with a laser printer, I could only print out black and white copies, which is fine for your first gig. Later, consider going full color, as you become more established and expect larger and better paid gigs. Here's the flyer I developed on the following page.

SUCCESS SECRETS IN EVERYDAY LIFE
with GINI GRAHAM SCOTT

Interviewed by Barbara Edwards, Business Coach
Former CEO of California Hosts

How You Can Apply Her Success Secrets in Your Everyday Life
Author of 200+ Books from Self-Help and Business to Novels and Kids Books.
Writer/Executive Producer of 10 Films
Lafayette Resident for 5 Years

Tuesday, October 1 - 6:30-8:30
Lafayette Library, Art & Discovery Room, 3491 Mt Diablo Blvd.
Sign Up at Eventbrite:
https://www.eventbrite.com/e/success-secrets-in-everyday-life-tickets-71942956319

Barbara Edwards will interview Gini about how she achieved her incredible career, based on not only writing and publishing books and producing films, but designing over two dozen published games, 100+ songs, and several dozen music videos.

> For the first time, see trailers for Gini's 6 latest films. Two feature over 30 Contra Costa Residents: *Me, My Dog, and I* and *The New Age of Aging*

Gini will also share her secret tips on how she was able to achieve so much and how you can do it, too, whatever your goals, hopes, and dreams. You can ask plenty of questions about her suggestions for you.

A Brief Bio:
Gini Graham Scott, Ph.D., CEO of Changemakers Publishing and Writing, is an internationally known writer, consultant, speaker, and workshop leader. Her recent books include *Increase Your Impact and Influence*, *Self-Publish Your Book in Multiple Formats*, and the *New World Neanderthals*. Her latest films include *The New Age of Aging*; *Me, My Dog, and I*; and *Rescue Me*. She has published 50+ books with major publishers and 150+ books through Changemakers Publishing on social trends, business, self-help, and for kids. She has worked with hundreds of clients as a ghostwriter for books and scripts, and is a communications strategist and consultant. Her website is www.changemakerspublishingandwriting.com.

Creating a Flyer for Future Events

Even if you don't have firm dates for future events, since you are waiting to see how the first event goes, you can create a flyer describing the next events you are planning. Then, if you have a large enough turn-out, you can schedule them and send out emails to attendees, as well as post them on various platforms, such as Eventbrite and Meetup. If you want to wait to schedule future events because of a low turnout, listing them on a flyer will provide a guide for what you might do next. For example, here's a copy of the flyer I prepared for possible future events.

DISCOVER NEW SECRETS OF SUCCESS AND HAVE FUN

UPCOMING PROGRAMS BY GINI GRAHAM SCOTT

Author of 200+ Books from Self-Help and Business to Novels and Kids Books. Writer/Executive Producer of 10 Films

Following are the next two topics in a series of talks:

December 5 - Increase Your Influence and Impact
Featuring New Ways to Share Your Message in Multiple Media
6:30-8:30 p.m. Location in Lafayette TBA

January 6 - What You Can Learn from Dogs
Featuring Special Advance Screenings of 2 New Films, *Me, My Dog, and I* and *Rescue Me;* and a new personality system based on discovering your Dog Type for more success in your life and work.
6:30-8:30 p.m. Location in Lafayette TBA

Sign up with your email for details on participating

Featuring....

Gini Graham Scott, Ph.D., CEO of Changemakers Publishing and Writing, an internationally known writer, consultant, speaker, and workshop leader. Her recent books include *Increase Your Impact and Influence*, *Self-Publish Your Book in Multiple Formats*, the *New World Neanderthals*, and *The Secret World of the Little Imps*. Her latest films include *The New Age of Aging*, *Me, My Dog, and I*, and *Rescue Me*. She has published over 50 books with major publishers and 150+ books through Changemakers Publishing on social trends, business, self-help, and for kids. She has worked with hundreds of clients as a ghostwriter for books and scripts, and as a communications strategist and consultant. Her website is www.changemakerspublishingandwriting.com.

If you are planning to create workshops based on the topic introduced at your first speaking event, create a flyer for this to hand out at your talk or use after your initial program. For instance, here's an example of a workshop flyer I created to hand out at my first program.

SUCCESS SECRETS IN EVERYDAY LIFE
with GINI GRAHAM SCOTT

Author of 200+ Books from Self-Help and Business to Novels and Kids Books. Writer/Executive Producer of 10 Films Lafayette Resident for 5 Years

A Workshop on How to Apply These Secrets in Your Everyday Life

Date and Time TBA - Sign Up with Your Email to Receive Details
Lafayette Library, Art & Discovery Room, 3491 Mt Diablo Blvd.

Gini will also share her secret tips on how she was able to achieve so much and how you can do it, too, whatever your goals, hopes, and dreams in your work and personal life. The program will draw on Gini's career experiences of over 40 years and cover topics such as:
- Turning failure into success
- Getting new ideas from your experiences
- Setting and achieving goals
- Increasing your creativity
- Using visualization to map out your path to success
- Prioritizing what you really want to do

The workshop will include discussion, interaction with others, visualization techniques, plenty of time for questions, and more.

A Brief Bio:
Gini Graham Scott, Ph.D., CEO of Changemakers Publishing and Writing, is an internationally known writer, consultant, speaker, and workshop leader. Her recent books include *Increase Your Impact and Influence*, *Self-Publish Your Book in Multiple Formats*, and the *New World Neanderthals*. Her latest films include *The New Age of Aging*; *Me, My Dog, and I*; and *Rescue Me*. She has published 50+ books with major publishers and 150+ books through Changemakers Publishing on social trends, business, self-help, and for kids. She has worked with hundreds of clients as a ghostwriter for books and scripts, and is a communications strategist and consultant. Her website is www.changemakerspublishingandwriting.com.

Announcing Your Event at Group Meetings

If you are a member of a networking, referral, or interest group, sometimes if you are new to the group, you may have a chance to announce your event, along with other information about what you do to the group. When you make such an announcement, ideally have your flyer to hand out to those who are interested. You might have sign-up forms to give out for individuals to take with them, too.

These are the following ways you might get to make an announcement:

- Everyone in the group briefly introduces themselves (a more common approach in smaller groups with 20 or fewer attendees).
- You bring a gift for the raffle, and can briefly say something about the prize, what you and your company do, and the event you want to announce.
- You win a prize in the raffle, and when you come forward to collect your prize, you can say something about yourself and your company and make your announcement.
- You have just joined the group and are invited to introduce yourself.
- You are a new attendee at a small group and other group members want to know who you are.

In making your announcement, you typically have about 15-30 seconds, though as much as 1 minute in some groups, usually with a smaller turn-out. To prepare for making this announcement, practice what is often called an "elevator speech." There are even presentations and workshops on creating a good elevator speech.

The big difference in your elevator pitch for your event is that you are using this brief time to highlight your event, as well as what your company does. The main points to highlight when you introduce yourself are these:

- Your name
- Your company name
- What you do to help and bring value to others
- How you help others through your event
- The title of your event
- The date, time, and location
- Where people can get more information

You can mention a website, but preferably have a flyer with this information to hand out to those interested or have the flyers available on a display table. If you have more than 30 seconds, you might add an interesting story about your company or something to be featured at your event. You can add some humor to spice up your announcement, if you are a good a storyteller.

Here's how I have typically made an announcement:

"Hi, everyone. I'm Gini Graham Scott with Changemakers Publishing and Writing. I help others increase their visibility and credibility by writing books, blogs, and scripts for them. I'm also starting a speaking series called Secrets of Success in Everyday Life to help people become more successful based on tips I learned along the way during my long career. The program's on Tuesday, October 1 at the Lafayette Library. I have flyers with me and on the display table, so you can learn more about this."

That announcement works out to about 80 words and 25 seconds. If I'm limited to 15 seconds, I drop some details. If I have a longer time, I show the flyer and a couple of books I have written.

Similarly, work out different versions of your announcement based on the time you have. The key is to keep your announcements short and to the point.

Announcing Your Event on the Social Media

If you already have a social media account on Facebook, Instagram, Twitter, or LinkedIn, you can post your event there, too. Later, you can do a more extensive social media campaign that might include ads, mostly notably on Facebook, Instagram, and Google. For now, just do some posts, and at most, boost a post to a local audience with a budget of $5 to $10 for a few days to see what kind of response you get. If people sign up for your event, not just like your post, you can increase your budget.

A good time to start your social media posts is about two weeks before the event. Then, write another post about your event every two or three days. This repetition will help your current followers or those who become followers due to your ads remember your event, since a one-time post can easily get lost in the mass of social media messages each day. Researchers have estimated that the average person sees 500 to 1000 posts zip by each day.

With any social media post, you want to keep it short -- even shorter than your copy on a flyer or event description. Include a photo, animated gif, or short video with your copy to attract attention. You want to quickly convey your message and include a link where those who are interested can learn more, such as by going to your Eventbrite link.

The key elements to include in your social media post are the title of your event and a few compelling bullet points to show the value from attending. Perhaps offer a free gift, such as a PDF with tips, for clicking a link to learn more. Also, include the date, time, location, and the link to click. In some cases, if you set up an event on an event platform like Eventbrite, the service will automatically post your event on selected social media, such as Facebook and Twitter. But don't rely on that single posting for results. Instead, create your own social media campaign with multiple posts, where you can repeat the same copy or vary it slightly, such with a different benefit of the event.

To illustrate, here's a sample post I created to promote my Success Secrets program.

Score a bullseye with Success Secrets in Everyday Life. Over 100 tips on how to gain more impact and influence and increase your sales and profits. On October 1, 6:30-8:30 at the Lafayette Library. Click below to learn more: https://www.eventbrite.com/e/success-secrets-in-everyday-life-tickets-71942956319

Then, as part of this campaign I planned to change the photo and some of the copy to encourage more awareness and impact, rather than repeating the same message each time.

Announcing Your Event on Your Website

If you have a website, this is another place to post your event. You can include your event announcement on your home page, or alternatively, create a line of two of copy to entice people to want to learn more about your event. Once they click for more information, you can include a more detailed description along with a link to register on your site using PayPal or a credit card, or send them to the event site to register, such as Eventbrite.

If you are effectively using SEO to increase the visibility of your site, people may find your site and event, if they are looking for products and services in a particular location. You can also use a gift incentive to encourage visitors to your site to provide their email to get the gift, such as a PDF of a book. Then, you send the gift to them at their email. Besides offering the gift, include a link to a site where people can RSVP for the event, such as on Eventbrite.

However, don't only expect people to find your site by searching for certain products or services. Use other methods to get people to visit your website, such as Facebook or Google ads, where you provide an incentive for people to go to your site. It's better to send them there rather than going directly to a separate event sign-up service, such as Eventbrite, because on your website, you can let them know about other things you are doing that might interest them. For instance, tell them more about what your company does to help clients, and briefly describe these different programs, services, or products. They just have to click a link to learn more.

Getting Announcements in Your Membership Organizations

If you belong to any membership organizations, many have a monthly newsletter, commonly in both a print and online edition. In either case, you can contact the editorial staff member handling the calendar or member news to get a posting. Some publications may even offer to feature you in a short article. If you place a small ad, often you will get a member discount.

Typically, these announcements will feature the link to sign up for your event, as well as contact information to connect with you directly. When you speak to the editor or newsletter coordinator, get the details for getting an announcement. In particular, find out the deadline to get in the next publication and the number of words or characters allowed to describe your event. Sometimes these are quite short -- only 100-150 words. Some publications will additionally invite you to send in a picture, which might be used in the posting.

For example, I got announcements of different lengths included in the online and printed newsletters of three Chambers of Commerce I belong to - Lafayette, Walnut Creek, and Danville, and I got announcements in the newsletter and on the website of a nearby writers' group.

Here's an example of such an announcement from the Lafayette Chamber Newsletter:

Advertising Your Event to the Venue's Audience

    Some venues have a newsletter or regular mailing to their members, and you can get listed in that. Sometimes these listings will be free or you can place an ad, following the venue's guidelines. Generally, it's best to place these listings or ads one or two weeks before your event, and possibly in both weeks.

    For example, for an additional $40, I placed a one-time ad in the Library's weekly newsletter two weeks before the event. Their guidelines indicated including a photo of a certain size along with the basic event information -- its title, date, and room in the library -- plus an event description of up to 100 words. Here's an example of this ad:

**Success Secrets in Everyday Life
with Gini Graham Scott**

Tuesday, Oct. 1, 2019
6:30 - 8:30 PM Arts & Science Discovery Center

Interviewed by Barbara Edwards, business coach, former California Hosts CEO. Gini, author of 200+ books, 10 feature films, will talk about how you can apply her success secrets in your everyday life. She'll share clips from her films on aging, dogs, and mysteries. Besides writing, she has a PhD, JD, 5 MAs, and helps clients write and publish books and scripts.

Presented by: Changemakers Publishing
Admission: $15 Eventbrite, $20 at door
Eventbrite: https://www.eventbrite.com/e/success-secrets-in-everyday-life-tickets-71942956319
More information: www.changemakerspublishingandwriting.com
Email: changemakerspub@att.net
Phone: (925) 385-0608

Setting Up a Table or Booth at a Local Trade Fair

Still another way to promote your event is through a table or booth at a local trade fair. It's probably not worth the cost to participate if you are only promoting a speaking gig. But if you plan to be at the fair to promote your products or services generally, you could additionally use the fair to attract attendees to your event.

The cost of participating in these fairs typically ranges from $100 to $300, a little less with an early bird discount. For a simple set-up, plan on having one or two large signs of about 18" x 44" on an easel. Design them with a few lines of copy to promote your product or service, and perhaps include your logo.

For instance, my signs included my company name and logo on top and my website on the bottom of the sign. In the center of the sign, the large, bold copy on one sign said: "Promote Your Business with the Social Media;" the copy on the other sign said: "We'll Write for You and Help You Get Published -- Books, Articles, Scripts, Blogs, and More!

Usually, you will get a 3 foot wide and 6 foot long table and sometimes a plain white covering. You will also get guidelines with details on how to set up, when to arrive, where to park, what to do if you need electricity or wi-fi access, and what to bring. You may also get suggestions on how to get more attendees to come to the fair.

For instance, here are the guidelines I got for participating in the Walnut Creek Business Trade Fair:

2019 Business TradeFaire

IMPORTANT GUIDELINES FOR EVENT DAY
Event Date: Tuesday, September 24, 2019 **Event Hours:** 5:00 - 7:00p.m.

Scott's Seafood Grill & Bar
1333 N California Blvd, Walnut Creek

Unloading your Booth Materials (Beginning at 3:00PM)
- Unload booth materials in front of Scott's on California Blvd. The unloading zone will be marked off with "No Parking" signs directly in front of the restaurant.
- Student helpers will be available to assist you.

Parking
- After you have finished unloading, please park in the **Locust Street parking garage**. Scott's will provide complimentary valet parking for attendees in their structure. They do not have sufficient spaces to accommodate their dinner guests, attendees, and exhibitors...and *we want to make it easy for the attendees*.

Set Up & Tear Down
- Exhibitor set up begins at 3:00 p.m. Booths must be fully constructed by 4:45p.m.
- You will receive your booth location upon checking in on event day.
- Each display area will include a skirted 6' table. Storage space is limited to under the tables.
- If you have an oversized (height or width) TradeFaire display, let us know before the event.
- Signage may be affixed to easels or skirting. Taping/stapling signage to walls or objects that may puncture or damage floors is not allowed.
- Please do not obstruct the visual access of other exhibitors.
- Have a prize drawing. This attracts people and provides you with business cards for follow-up after the show. To encourage attendees to return, hold your drawing at 6:30 p.m. and post the names of the winners at your booth.
- **All booths must be staffed from 5:00 to 7:00 p.m. Booths may not be dismantled until after 7:00p.m.**

Electricity
- Electricity is available only if you ordered it in your registration form. <u>If you requested electricity, remember to bring your own extension cords.</u>

WI – FI Access
We have been advised that Wi-Fi is available at the restaurant; however, may not be strong enough to support all of the exhibitors. You may want to consider using your phone as a hotspot. (also known as Wi-Fi tethering)

INCREASE TRADEFAIRE ATTENDANCE BY GETTING THE WORD OUT
- Invite your customers, prospects, family, and friends to visit you at your TradeFaire booth.
- Use Facebook, Twitter, email, and mailings. Entice attendees with a prize or special offer.
- Just think, if each exhibitor brought ten attendees to the event...there would be an **additional 500 attendees**.

REMINDER: Exhibitors selling products or services from their booth must complete and return the attached Sellers Agreement required by the State Board of Equalization.

Ideally, bring your own dark colored covering, such as in black, dark blue, or brown, so your display better stands out. You can use table easels to feature products or flyers about your products and services. Bring a bowl to collect business cards. Many exhibitors also bring a bowl of candy, cookies, or snacks to attract attendees. Some offer a drawing for a prize, usually a sample product or coupon for an introductory service.

Other items to include in your display are:
- Samples of your product
- Brochures about your product or service
- Business cards
- Index cards and a pen for attendees who don't have business cards

Additionally, bring flyers about your event. Generally, you only need 20 to 25 copies of your flyers and other handouts, since only a small percentage of the attendees will take flyers, since they aren't interested or don't want to carry the material around with them. For instance, at the Walnut Creek Business Trade Show, there were about 150 attendees, and I gave out 20 flyers. But rather than pick up materials, many attendees will offer business cards or write down their contact information on index cards. Then, you can follow up later with those who express interest in attending your speaking event or in talking to you about your other products or services.

Preferably stand at your table or get up from your chair when people come by, so you appear friendly and enthusiastic. As people glance your way, greet them with a smile and "Hello." Invite people to look at your display and take flyers. As appropriate, mention that you are speaking on a topic that they might find of interest and hand them a flyer.

Ideally, arrive at the beginning of the set-up time to set up your table or booth, since it will usually be easier to find parking to unload your equipment. Coming early will also give you time to visit the other exhibitors after you set up your booth before the fair starts. After you introduce yourself, you may find that some exhibitors are interested in what you are doing. Some may visit you at your booth later.

Then, it's show time for the fair, which usually lasts for two or three hours.

Contacting the Local Media

Finally, you can promote your event through the local media. To do so, create a list of the print and online publications in your area which include announcements about local events and articles about local residents and activities. For each publication, list the publisher, managing or executive editor, and the editor of the section where you want to pitch your listing or article. If you aren't sure which editor to target, when several editors handle features, news stories, and events, you can call the office to ask which editor to contact. Alternatively, you can send your article or press release to all of the contacts and later indicate you weren't sure who to contact. An editor can advise you who to contact in the future.

Prepare two types of announcements:

- a listing and short description of your event for the publication's calendar or events section; provide a JPEG of a photo or your logo if these listings include this.

- a longer article of 300 to 500 words, written like a press release, if the publication features such articles.

You can additionally include a short cover letter to indicate what you are sending.

In general, it is best to send information to the local media in writing rather than calling before you send it to let the editor know you are sending something or calling afterwards to find out if the editor got it. Often editors are quite busy and, with some exceptions, they prefer to get any information about events and local news in writing rather than have phone calls. Many don't answer their phones or return messages left on voice mail. An exception might be if you meet an editor at a business networking event or trade fair.

When you write, the usual practice is to include information in the body of the email, rather than sending an attachment, since editors are generally reluctant to open emails with attachments they aren't expecting from someone they don't know, due to fears about viruses and other malware. But if you write first and the editor asks you to send more information or a photo, you can include an attachment.

Check on the deadlines for when to send your information. Usually, a week or two in advance is fine for newspapers or newsletters. For monthly magazines, check when the deadline is for the following month, and submit your announcement, article, or press release before that.

When you send in any publicity materials, there are no guarantees, unlike ads where you pay in advance and schedule a placement for a certain time. Whether your publicity materials get printed depend on the editor's interest and available spacing. So send it off and hope for the best. As for advertising, it generally is too expensive to advertise a first time gig in local publications, aside from placing an ad in the newsletter of the venue hosting your gig.

CHAPTER 5: PUTTING ON YOUR EVENT

Now that it is almost time to put on your event, there are some things to think about in the few days before, during, and immediately after your event.

The Final Count-Down Before Your Event

To make sure your event goes well, here are some things to do shortly before the event to prepare:
- Create a checklist of all the things you will bring to the event if you haven't already done so. If you have already created a checklist, as described in Chapter 2, review it to be sure you have done everything on it or add anything else you want to include now.
- Double check that you have all the items on your checklist, including any flyers, business cards, products to display, sign-up forms, clipboards, refreshments, and a cash box.
- A day or two before your event, take all the items you plan to bring to the event to a central location. This will help to show what you already have and what you still need. Also, having everything in this central place will enable you to quickly take these items to the event.
- A week or so before the event, double check with the individual making the arrangements at the selected venue to see that everything is moving ahead as expected. If you have to make a final payment to confirm your booking, make it now.
- A few days before the event, check with the individuals participating in the event with you, such as the person handling sign-ins or introducing you, to be sure they will still be there. If you have arranged for a videographer, check that he or she is still planning to come. As necessary, make other arrangements to handle the assignments for those who can't attend.
- A day or two before the event, double check that the individuals participating in the event are still coming as planned, and there are no illnesses or other problems that might interfere with their participation. If necessary, make last minute arrangements, if possible, to take on the responsibilities of those who won't be there.
- If the individuals coming to the event need directions, send them this information. If they are coming at a time when they might expect traffic, advise them that they may encounter some delays, so they can leave earlier and arrive on time.
- A day or two before the event, buy any snacks and beverages you plan to have at the event or arrange for someone to buy these items for you. Estimate how much to bring based on how many people you expect. Gather the necessary number of platters,

dishes, cups, glasses, napkins, and paper plates to serve attendees. Preferably, pick up food items you might eat or drink later in case you end up with leftovers. For example, for the Success Secrets event at the Lafayette Library, I planned on about a dozen attendees, since I had six paid sign-ups and thought another half-dozen attendees might show up at the door. Thus, the day before the event, I picked up two boxes of cookies and two gallons of tea at the supermarket, and I brought two dozen napkins, plates and cups from home.

- Print out the names of the individuals who have signed-up and paid on Eventbrite and the names of anyone who has signed up through Meetup or other platforms. Place the names and lists of the individuals who signed up under your checklist and sign-ups printouts, so anyone at the door can check who has already paid and collect payments from those who are signing in at the door.

- Review what you plan to say in your presentation. If you are doing a presentation with someone else, review what you plan to say together. Then, practice your presentation, as necessary.

- The day before the event, check with the individual in charge of the venue that everything is or will be set up as planned

- Print out any forms and flyers you need.
- Plan to bring a camera or your phone to take pictures.

What to Do the Day of the Event

- In the morning, make a last minute call to the individual in charge of the venue and to others helping you to put on the program to make sure everything is still going ahead as planned.
- Allow enough time to pack everything in your car or other transportation.
- Pack everything you need and go.

It's a Set-Up

Generally, you will have about 15 to 30 minutes to set up for your event before your official start time. Figure on some attendees coming 5 to 10 minutes early, so be ready to greet them and sign them in. If necessary, use some of the networking time -- about 15-20 minutes -- to finish your set up.

First, set up your sign-in table with the following:
- sign-in forms
- a list or print-out of the individuals who have already RSVPed and paid
- a cash box
- any separate forms for credit card payments, if you are able to take these.

The sign-in table might also include your business cards and flyers for upcoming events and any product or service specials you are offering to attendees. If this is a large group with a dozen or more attendees, you can have name badges and a pen or sharpie for people to fill out the badges. If a small group, name tags aren't necessary.

Next, set up your display table with whatever you have brought to display, such as samples of products, flyers, and brochures about your products or services. If you are using any easels to display posters, set them up.

Set up a separate table or section of your display table for refreshments, along with any cups, plates, and napkins.

Additionally, check that everything for your presentation is set up and in working order. This includes checking that the venue organizer has set out the chairs or set them up yourself. If you are using a laptop, projector and screen, check that this system works. If you are using a flash drive with a PowerPoint or video, set this up so this is ready to go, and if necessary, check that you can readily switch from one PowerPoint or video to another. Sometimes the venue will have one or two techs who can help you check the equipment. If so, let them set up the system and see that everything works. If necessary, improvise if you can't get everything to work, such as by passing out handouts of your PowerPoint slide show and referring to your handout as you talk about different slides.

If you have arranged for a videographer to record your presentation, he or she should make sure that the camera and mics are ready to go and let you know when they are. If there are any background distractions, like colorful posters on the wall, the videographer should let you know, so you can move them or cover them up.

For example, during the set up period for my program, the videographer noticed two sinks behind either side of the stage, which would make for a weird background. Fortunately, I had a brown blanket in the car which I used to cover them up. If that hadn't worked, we would have had to move the podium and chairs for the interview, so I wouldn't have sinks on either side of my head as I spoke. Then, that crisis averted, the videographer set up a wireless mic between me and Barbara. While he had considered switching back and forth to show Barbara while she asked her questions, he decided that it would be better for her to ask her questions off camera and only film my responses.

Finally, arrange for someone to take photos of your event with your camera or phone, so you can later post them on the social media or otherwise use them in promoting your next event. You can take some photos during or after you set up, such as of the display table, sign-in table, and the whole room. Additionally, ask someone to take a few photos of you doing your talk, even if you have to simulate doing this. If you have a videographer, the videographer might do this or later pull some photos from the video. Or you can create screenshots of selected video images.

Once everything is set up, focus on welcoming the attendees. Ideally, have someone at the door about 15 minutes before the program starts to greeting people.

Greeting Attendees and Networking

As attendees arrive, whoever is at the door should greet them warmly and check if they have registered by looking at the sign-up list or printout of attendees. Invite attendees to pick up any material at the sign-in table, and point out the tables with refreshments and items on display.

Attendees can be free to do their own networking and stake out their seats for the program. Once everything at the sign-in table is under control with at least one person to sign in arrivals, you and others putting on the program can mingle with the arriving attendees. Introduce yourself and say that you will be presenting the program. Answer any questions the person may have and move on to the next attendee. Should you notice any commonalties among attendees as you go around networking, you can introduce the attendees to each other. Consider this networking period a way to warm up the audience by helping everyone feel more engaged in attending your event.

Putting on Your Presentation

About two to three minutes before your presentation, you or someone from your team should announce that the program is about to get started, so attendees should take their seats. Most or all attendees will do so, and once everyone is seated, you can begin the presentation.

Usually, begin with someone -- preferably a team member other than the main presenter -- making opening remarks about what to expect at the program. This person might also announce some house rules, such as the location of the restrooms, and then introduce the presenters.

For example, at the Success Secrets event, Barbara Edwards, who would be interviewing me before showing the Success Secrets video, handled the introductions. She warmly welcomed everyone and explained that she would be interviewing me about my experiences that led me to a number of insights about what to do to be successful and I would answer questions about that. After that, we would show the video.

Then, she sat down and asked me a series of questions. The plan was to ask me questions for 20 minutes, show a 12 minute video with six trailers of films I wrote and produced, ask me more questions for another 20 minutes, and end with the 12 minute Success Secrets video, followed by about 15 minutes of audience questions. After the first interview segment, the venue's tech team started the first video with six trailers and left, thinking everything would go well.

And for the first half of the presentation, it did. Barbara and I had already gone over the questions she would ask and my expected answers, so I generally responded as expected, as the videographer recorded her off-camera questions and my on-camera responses. Meanwhile, the attendees listened quietly and seemed genuinely interested in what I was saying, so I relaxed as I talked.

Then, a big technical glitch occurred that we hadn't prepared for. After the tech team had set up the first 12 minute film trailers video to be ready to go at the push of a button, they expected that I only had to click one button to go to the YouTube home screen and click another button to start the second video, which was initially on the top of the video display panel on the right of the screen. But the techs didn't realize that the YouTube display panel would change, so I now saw different videos in the display. As a result, I couldn't immediately find the second video, and as we searched on YouTube to find it for about five minutes, many attendees left. It took so long to find it, because we had to locate the right channel and the exact name under which the video was posted.

Thus, it's really important to fully check out any PowerPoints and videos you are planning to show. You need to have the right equipment to show them or have a list of the YouTube links to the videos you plan to feature. Don't think you can easily find these links on YouTube in the middle of your presentation.

Finally, at the end of your formal presentation, invite audience members to ask any questions, and allow about 10-15 minutes for questions.

After your presentation ends, thank everyone for coming. Invite them to visit the display table and help themselves to any refreshments that are still remaining.

After It's All Over

Once your program is over, thank anyone who helped out and pack up everything to take back with you. If some people can stay to help you, great.

If you have a videographer creating a video for you, go over the next steps, such as when you can see the raw footage and how you can arrange to have the footage edited to create the final video.

Then, it's over -- your first speaking gig. Now you can go home, relax, and put everything away. Later, you can think about how to use your accomplishment and any video for future gigs, webinars, online courses, and more. It doesn't matter if you had a low turnout or if glitches occurred in your presentation. You can still use putting on your presentation and what you learned from the process to help you with the programs you want to do in the future.

But for now, it's all over. So just CHILL and RELAX!

CHAPTER 6: DEVELOPING A PROMOTIONAL VIDEO FROM YOUR EVENT

If you had a videographer record your event, you can work with the videographer to create a promotional video or series of videos to use in the future. Even if you encounter problems in working with this videographer, you can still use the raw footage or initially edited footage to edit by yourself or with the help of a video editor. In this editing process, you can create one or more videos to promote your products or services and help you get your next speaking gigs.

Getting Ready for the Video Shoot

To work most effectively with your videographer, know in advance what you want, although this can change as you get more feedback on ways to use these videos.

Typically, the videographer will ask for a payment for the initial video session (about $75-125 an hour) plus a payment for editing, which includes your feedback on what to edit in your first review (about $100-200 for this). Should you want additional editing, expect to pay for this on an hourly basis. Even if the videographer wants to quit after the first edit, since not all videographers are video editors, get the footage from the unedited video, the first edit, or both. Then, you can bring in a video editor to complete the edit, which is what I did.

As previously noted, you commonly have to pay for the video shooting when the videographer arrives or finishes shooting the video at your presentation, though sometimes you will be asked to pay the full amount upfront when you hire the videographer, though I don't advise this, since you can be stuck if the videographer doesn't show up or you don't like the results. Another possibility is paying one-third to one-half down on hiring the videographer, another one-third to one-half when the videographer shoots the video, and the last third or an additional payment for editing -- commonly before the first edit, though sometimes you pay this after the videographer submits the edit. In my case, I paid the videographer in full for shooting the video and the first edit when he arrived. Rather than waiting for him to ask or until the end of the shoot, I gave him the check right away, which he appreciated. And that's what I recommend, paying the amount due when the videographer arrives to show your good faith that the videographer will do a good job.

When the videographer sets up, he or she will ask you about what to shoot. This will minimally include the podium, platform, or table where you will be speaking. Additionally, the shoot may include your display table, and if you have a large enough crowd, the attendees.

The videographer will also want to set the audio level for your speaking, which means testing the mic and setting the volume by asking you and everyone who will be in the presentation to speak into the mic several times in order to can get the volume right. In some cases, this mic set-up will involve moving the mic between the presenters to adjust for one person speaking more loudly or softly than the other. Or if the videographer has more than one mic, each speaker can have a mic. In my case, the videographer used one mic on the table between me and Barbara, and he moved it closer to me so my answers would be louder, while her questions sounded like they were off in the distance.

The videographer should also check the background to make sure nothing is interfering with a shot focused on the main speakers. If it is, as previously noted, you need to remove anything that's interfering or cover it up, as I did with the sinks in the room in the library.

Also, discuss if you want to videographer to film the audience if it is large enough. If so, let those in the audience know, so they can move to the rear of the seating area, if they don't want to be in a shot. In larger events that are being videotaped, the organizers often have a waiver form that attendees must sign to indicate they understand and agree that they may be videotaped at the program; although if they don't want to be filmed, they can tell the videographer not to include them and move out of the way. But at your first presentation if you only have a small number of attendees, it is easier to informally explain that you are videotaping your presentation, so anyone who doesn't want to be in the video can move to the back row. If you don't plan to videotape the audience, explain that the videographer will only film your speaking program.

Finally, go over with the videographer what else you expect to be in the video besides your presentation. Commonly, this will include what's on the display table and possibly a shot of your flyer about the event. If the videographer plans to shoot the display after the speaking program, leave it up when you pack after the event so the videographer can film it. Otherwise, you have to quickly put up your display again to include it in the video, which is what happened after my program. After all the books were packed in boxes, I had to quickly unpack them and set up the book display again.

Once it's time for the presentation, you or the program announcer should introduce the videographer and explain that he will now begin filming the presentation. Then, you are ready to go.

Planning the Edit

Once the filming is over, discuss the editing arrangements with the videographer. You can provide a general idea of what you want, such as indicating that you want the display to go in the beginning of the video and that you want to insert other videos in the middle or at the end. It's best to send your specific instructions for editing in writing, after you have seen the raw footage so you can indicate what you want to cut or change by referring to the time codes on the video player.

While you can trust some videographers to be effective when you ask them to make the best cuts to make a shorter video, such as cutting 40 minutes of video to 20 minutes, other videographers ask you to be very precise about what to cut. And by precise, they mean they want you to give them the second on the timeline where to start and end each cut.

In addition, the videographer may ask you to send in some copy for titles to go in the beginning, at the end, and at certain transitions. To Illustrate, here is the listing of what to include which I sent to the videographer, along with instructions on where to insert each item.

<u>Suggested Copy for Transitions In Video (White Type On Black Background)</u>

1) Initial title for video:
    Success Secrets in Everyday Life
    A Presentation by Gini Graham Scott
2) Image of the flyer for the event (though maybe just top half or two thirds of it, since it will be difficult to read the bio on the bottom and the copy about Barbara Edwards. Use your judgment on how much to include.
3) Shot of the book display
4) Initial part of the interview with me
5) Transition slide for the video of the six films. Use this title:
    Trailers of Feature Films, Documentaries, and TV Pilots
    by Gini Graham Scott and Changemakers Productions
6) The rest of interview with me
7) Transition slide for Success Secrets Video. Use this copy:
    The Success Secrets in Everyday Life Video
    Featuring Over 100 Tips You Can Apply In Your Work and Personal Relationships
8) A credits List (take out Barbara Edward's website, since there is no website)
9) Final Contact Information (you can repeat what's in the last slide of the Success Secrets Video

Usually, the videographer will send you the raw footage of the video to review in a platform like Dropbox or on their website, where you can watch the video online or download it to view on your computer. Preferably, download the video to your computer, so you have the original footage if you need it.

You'll see the seconds on the timeline when you play the video. However, even indicating the second to make or end a cut isn't exact, because the time can vary by a fraction of a second in either direction. Thus, it's best to include a few words indicating where you want the cut to begin and end.

Sometimes it can be a little difficult to review a video online to determine the times for making the cuts, because on some online platforms, when you stop and start the video, it can go back to the beginning. If that happens, you have to move the timeline indicator under the video to just before you made a cut to start the video again. Thus, if this happens, for every minute of video, allow about two or three minutes to write down the times for beginning and end of a cut.

Alternatively, if you can download the video and view it in a video player, such as Windows Media Player or Camtasia, you won't have that problem and can really stop and restart the video without losing your place.

To illustrate, here's how I provided the videographer with a series of cuts from the beginning to the end of the video. I divided the listing of cuts into two sections to indicate the first half of cuts for the first 20 minutes before the film trailers video and the second half after this video to the end of my presentation before a final video.

COMMENTS ON CUTS IN VIDEO - To 29.17

Here is the first half of my comments to 29.17. I have tried to note the seconds as closely as possible, but they might be slightly off.

1) Increase sound level slightly on opening pan of books.

2) Try to cut this to 60 seconds from about 2 minutes. The main reason for cuts are there is a bright flash on the book and I have tried to focus on the business, self-help, and books about writing.
    About .10 or .11 - take out book with bright flash
    Take out New Middle Ages, Back to the Middle Ages, How Rich Kill -- .20 to about .27
    Take out More Success and Happiness due to flash .30-.32
    Take out Dealing with Copyright book .55-56 (overly technical book)
    Take out Trial and You the Jury 1.01-1.04
    Take Out Discovering Your Dog Type, You the Jury, What's Your Dog Type 1:22-1:24
    Take Out What's Your Dog Type Again 1:53
Can you make title for Barbara Edwards stand out more --about 2:03, 2:40-2:44. Maybe use Gold to stand out from white background.
Take out reference to Middle East clients and their families 2:50-2:58
Take out reference to largest dissertation 3:11-3:20
Take out reference to scary experience in studying group 3:49-4:17 (story too long)
Take out references to going to do participation observation of MLM group 4:52-5:15
    (story goes on too long) Just say I wrote a series of books
Take out reference to writing spiral bound books 5:29-5:52 (too much detail)
Take out where closed my eyes and turn to Barbara to ask more questions 5:53-5:56;
    maybe continue to take out until 6:04
Take out story about polygraph examiner 7:01-7:52 (too much detail)
Talk about the panel on Oprah okay. Start with question on how you do books so fast.

Take out reference to books 8:51-8:57
Take out references to marijuana 9:05-9:24, but leave in comment that I could flip into an altered state at any time.
Take out reference to dreams, Oh Peg It, and going around the country 9:46-10:53;
Take out some of detail about my moving experience. 11:08 to 11:38
Start with "I had a very crazy management company, and include line, so I felt I was in a movie, keep I called it moving on.
Take out detail about story 11:58-12:40
At 15:01 after Barbara asks how did I get into films, I'd like to just keep in "I decided to go pro and moved to Lafayette at the time
Take out 15:03-15:24
Take out 15:47-17:15 - Drop story about problem with woman filmmaker
Start with I met this actor at 17:15
Take out film 17:34-29:17.

COMMENTS ON CUTS IN VIDEO - From 29.17 to the End

Here is the second half of my comments from 29.17 to the end. I have tried to note the seconds as closely as possible, but they might be slightly off.

Delete 29.16 to 29.26. Start with "What are the major challenges you faced."
    Leave in the section about conflict resolution
Delete 30.59 to 31.13
    Cut section on my writing about different experiences to being an entrepreneur
Delete 31:43 to 33.18
    Start with I always did all sorts of things
Delete 33:30 to 33:53
    Start with question about if I want to write a book
Delete 34:02 to 34:17 (mix-up about the book title)
    Start with comment: "There are all these platforms, end with "I combined all these things together"
Delete 35:42 to 35:57
    Start with this started off as a PowerPoint presentation
Delete 36:57 to 37:04
    Start with "There are some writers in the group."
    End with that's what I started doing with a lot of my books
Delete 38:26-39.29
    Start with "There are a lot of niche publishers.
From 39:55-40:00 I make a comment about how I make more writing my own books.
    What do you think? Should I leave that in or cut that.
Delete 40.00-42.10
    Then pick up Success Secrets Video.

After you provide these detailed cuts for the videographer, if these are done correctly, that completes the project. To determine if they are correct, review the edited video on Dropbox, on the videographer's website, or download it, to make sure the videographer has made the edits correctly. If not, the videographer should make further corrections for any mistakes without additional charges. although in the spirit of good will, you might offer to pay for any changes.

What do you do if the videographer doesn't follow all of your instructions and refuses to do anymore, even if you offer to pay for future changes? Then, you have to find a video editor, who may also be a videographer. That's what happened to me after my videographer made a series of mistakes and then announced: "I'm done."

The first mistake was that the videographer didn't see my first half of my corrections and didn't ask me about it, when I said I was sending the second half of the corrections. Additionally, he missed a few requested edits in the second half, and he cut out a couple of sections that I indicated should remain in the video. Finally, when I asked him to change the lower-third titling for an introduction to another color, such as gold, since he used hard-to-read white lettering against a black and white background, he used a garish orange color.

Thus, I wrote to him asking him to do another edit, explaining that he had missed making cuts in the first half and telling him how to fix the incorrect cuts in the second half. But now the videographer refused to make any more cuts, even though I offered to pay for the extra time.

Fortunately, I had already downloaded the cut video, now 36 minutes, down from 56 minutes, so I could give that to another video editor. But there was no way to recapture what he cut out by mistake from the original edit, since he had deleted that. This is why you should download and keep the original footage before the videographer makes any edits. At least, my videographer did have a copy of the raw files from his camera which the video editor could open, though I couldn't provide precise timing for the desired cuts, since I couldn't view the raw files myself.

In any case, that editing problem was a good learning experience in how to work with a videographer, and I soon found a video editor from my business contacts who was able to complete the video.

Determining How to Cut Your Video

Despite the tumultuous break with my original videographer, the upside was I discovered that I should cut the video footage into a series of short videos -- not just make a single 30 minute video. And if my videographer balked at making additional edits to create a single video, he would have certainly resisted making multiple videos, which I now wanted to us on the social media and on my website to help promote future programs.

Making a variety of videos is something to consider in making your own video. A longer 20 to 30 minute video may be fine for showing at a future program, such as presenting this after a brief introduction to the program, and following it with questions, discussion, and group interaction inspired by the video.

But for promotional purposes, you can cut the longer video into a series of two to three minute segments to feature in promotions. A good way to use them is to post each shorter video on YouTube. Then, select the relevant short video file or link to the video to send to a prospective client. Or you can post the link to a short video on Facebook, Instagram, Twitter, or other social media, and feature a link to a different video with each post. Still another way to use these shorter video segments is by linking to the video with a series of blogs or press releases or by embedding a link from YouTube on a page on your website. Then, a visitor can click on a thumbnail to go the YouTube video posting.

For example, here's how I cut up my own 30 minute video into these segments.

SUGGESTIONS FOR SHORT VIDEO CLIPS

Here are suggestions for short videos and the titles for them to be created in addition to the longer 30 minute video with 12 minutes of my Success Secrets video and 18 minutes of highlights from my complete talk. Titles can be changed if you suggest something better. When doing a dissolve, use a black dissolve or jump cut, rather than a dissolve with different images as you'll see around 16.48.

1) Introducing Success Secrets in Everyday Life
    Display of books 08.17-1.05
    1:05-1:10, flyer,
    1:10-1:33 Barbara's Introduction (about 1 ½ minutes)

2) How Can You Write So Many Books?
    1:37-1.44 How can you write so many books
        Cut out the section where I close my eyes
    1:55-2.52 Could write really quickly… to "into popular books
        Cut discussion about magicians
     3:30-5:03 "So that was my second book called the Magicians… to "so one thing
        led to another (about 2 minutes and 50 seconds)

3) Experiencing a Few Minutes of Fame
    5:06-6:20 I know you were on Oprah…to "I was on several other shows about lying
        Cut details about other shows, polygraph examiner
    7:00-7:31 Then on the show there was a panel…to "It was fun being the expert on
        Oprah" (about 1 ¾ minutes)

4) Using a Creative Process to Be More Productive
   7:34 to 8:14   Tell Me what kind of process you use...to "I would get in this altered state of consciousness
   Cut reference to marijuana
   8:35-8:42 I could just flip into this altered state...to "Helpe me experience that."
   (about 1 minute)

5) Becoming a Game Designer
   8:43-9:00   There was a point with a boyfriend...to "I started having dreams."
   (cut reference to Oh Peg It)
   9:24-10:01 So I started going around the country to different toy manufacturers...to "running companies in the early 60s
   (about 1 minute)

6) How Did You Start to Write Scripts?
   10:04-11:40   How did you start writing scripts..."It was kind of a crazy thing"
   (about 1 ½ minutes)

7) How Did You Learn to Turn Your Scripts into Movies?
   11:51-14:23   So how did you learn how to turn your scripts into movies... to "So I started doing professional work"
   14:30-14:57   From that....to "So I started going to film funding conferences."
   16:28-16:48   Then I met one of the actors... to "Turning that into a film."
   (about 3 1/4 minutes - you could leave out the last 20 minutes if hard to include)

CHAPTER 7: USING YOUR FIRST EVENT TO GET OTHER GIGS

After you put on your first event, you can use this in a number of ways to prepare for and promote other gigs and get paid for them.

Review Your Event to Improve for the Future

After your event is over, review what happened to see how you can improve for the future. In doing so, consider the following:
- How did your preparations go for what to bring?
- How did the arrangements work out with the venue you selected?
- How did things go when you arrived to set up for the event?
- How do you feel about the presentation?
- How effective was your marketing and promotion of the event?
- What can you do to make each aspect of the presentation better?

In other words, go over what you did from developing the program to presenting it to assess what you did and what you can do better next time. In doing this assessment, rate each thing that happened on a scale of 1 to 10, and think about what you can do to improve anything with a rating of less than 8 or 9. You can use the chart on page 95 to help you do your assessment.

For example, when I did this assessment, I thought of the many things that went wrong and noted the following:
- I didn't use a checklist and forgot to do a number of things in setting up the event, so I resolved to have a checklist the next time.
- In selecting the venue, I didn't carefully observe the room, since I was focused on determining if the laptop and projector set up would work. So I didn't notice there were two sinks with faucets in the front of the room.
- I didn't allow enough time for choosing a videographer, since I kept waiting to determine if there would be enough sign-ups to go forward with the event. I didn't realize that I could use a video of the event regardless of the turn-out. As a result, I scrambled to quickly find a videographer in a week. Though I lucked out in finding a competent videographer who was available at a reasonable price, I could have easily have ended up not finding a videographer or having to pay a much higher amount.
- I didn't properly test out the technology and make the necessary arrangements to use it. I also didn't bring a print-out of the links to the videos to show on YouTube, resulting in a mad scramble to find them during the presentation.

- Though I had all of the refreshments prepared at home ready to go – two boxes of cookies, cups, and a jug of cold tea, I left the tea in the refrigerator, since I didn't have a list of items to bring.

- I rambled on too long in giving some of my responses to interview questions at the presentation. Though I had written out my answers, I didn't review them or practice the answers before the presentation. Instead, I answered with the first thing that came to mind, which was satisfactory, but too long. After that I realized I would have to spend more time timing, polishing, and shortening my responses in a future presentation.

Deciding What to Change

Based on your assessment of any problems in your presentation, decide how to fix them in the future. For example:

- If you didn't use a checklist, make one and go over it to check that you are including everything you need for future presentations.

- If there were problems with the venue, go over any problems with the venue organizer to see if you can fix those in the future, or consider using a different venue in the future.

- If you want to use a videographer in the future, review any problems with your first videographer and see if these can be corrected or allow plenty of time to find another videographer and review their work, pricing, and arrangements to help you make your selection.

- If you had problems in working with the technology, see how you can better set up the system or bring in a person to coordinate the technology for you in the future.

Most importantly, polish up your presentation. If you had the program videotaped, apart from using the video to help you find gigs in the future, review the video to help you assess what worked well and what can be improved. Go over the video with an associate or coach to help you make the assessment and use that assessment to guide the changes you make. Possibly, you may find that you need a professional coach to help with your speaking. If so, showing this person the video can help them determine what to correct to help you improve.

As you notice things to change, work out a plan for implementing these improvements. After that, practice what you want to do differently and better.

In short, figure out what to improve based on your assessment of any problems in preparing or putting on your presentation. Then, set up a schedule for what you will do -- and DO IT!

Review of Presentation			
Assessment	Rating	What's Wrong If Anything	How To Fix Problem
Equipment Needed			
Materials for Presentation			
Items to Display			
Promotional Materials			
Sign-Up Table Material			
Handouts and Evaluation Forms			
Refreshments			
My Presentation			

Use Your Video to Promote Your Presentation

If you have created a video of your presentation, you can use it in various ways to find other gigs. To do so, have it edited it into a series of formats to use in pitching your program to different audiences.

If your videographer isn't a skilled editor, which is why my videographer called it quits after I submitted my list of edits, find a video editor to help you. Sometimes your videographer may recommend an editor, which mine did, or you may have other contacts who can edit videos, though they aren't full-time editors. That's what I did, since my website designer was a video editor, too. Alternatively, you may find leads to a video editor through your network of business contacts, or post a request for an editor on your neighborhood online forum. Other ways to find an editor include Craigslist, Upwork, and Fiverr. To help you decide who to hire, review examples of previous videos the editor has edited, and ask about pricing and availability. Commonly, editing costs range from $50 to $100 an hour.

To guide the editor, think of the ways you can use different versions of your video. Some recommended formats are:
- a 20-30 minute video with highlights of your full presentation.
- 1-3 minute promotional videos featuring different topics you discuss.

Each video should begin with a title and end with your contact information. You can include credits for the videographer, video editor, venue, and anyone else involved in putting on your program in your 20-30 minute video. But skip the credits on your short promotional videos; just include your title and contact information, since this video is too short for credits.

Upload these different versions to your YouTube channel, so you can provide the links to prospects who might hire you to speak, be on a panel, or put on a seminar, workshop, or webinar. The videos can also be embedded on your website, such as on a page devoted to your speaking programs.

Using Photos from Your Event in Your Promotional Materials

You can use photos of your event in your press releases or pitch letters to get gigs. It doesn't matter if you had low attendance. Don't show the crowd. Just focus on photos of you doing the presentation, along with any display material that contributes to your credibility.

These photos can be taken by a camera or phone. Or if a videographer creates a video for you, he or she can give you some still images from the video. You can leave the selection up to the videographer after you provide general guidelines on what to include (i.e.: a few images of you talking enthusiastically about the subject). To be even more precise about what to include, indicate the second on the timeline where the image to turn into a photo appears. The videographer will then send you a .JPG for each photo. Another way to get photos from a video is to play the video on your computer and take some screen shots of selected images. Then, turn them into .JPG files. Once you get these .JPG files, you can include these phots on your website or in press releases and social media postings.

Creating Promotional Materials

After your program is over, you can create your promotional materials featuring the program you have already done and what you plan to do in the future. Use a photo from your event on your release or flyer for future events.

If you have created a short video or series of promotional videos from your program, use a link to one of these videos for your social media. Pick the one that is most relevant for each release or social media posting. If you are doing a pitch to the media, link to one of the short one to three minute promotional videos, since those working in the media have a short attention span. But if you are doing a pitch to a prospective client, use a link to your longer video to provide a better idea of how you do a presentation, and perhaps include a link to one or two relevant promotional videos.

The types of promotional materials to create are the following:
- a flyer with a photo from your first gig to hand out to your interest, business, and networking groups to indicate that you are looking for speaking gigs,
- a flyer with a photo from your first gig if you are planning any workshops based on your initial speaking program,
- a blog on your subject with a photo in which you talk about your first gig and indicate you are looking for future speaking gigs. Include a link to a promotional video.
- a press release for the local media noting that you have recently given the first of many speaking programs on this topic and you will be speaking to groups. (List a few examples of the type of organizations you plan to contact. Indicate if you have set up any gigs for the future. If your topic relates to a subject in the news or of special local concern, highlight this in your release.)
- a series of short social media posts with photos.

In the case of flyers, you can create a more professionally-designed flyer with graphics, if you have the budget for this or are a designer yourself. I have just created simple flyers in Word to demonstrate how you might create the copy for such a flyer.

To illustrate, here are examples which I created to promote future Success Secrets programs.

A Flyer to Get Speaking Gigs

This is a simple flyer I created in WORD listing several topics I could speak about. It notes a previous program I conducted to establish credibility for doing future programs, before listing the topics for future programs.

WANT A SPEAKER ON NEW WAYS TO ACHIEVE SUCCESS?

SPEAKING PROGRAMS BY GINI GRAHAM SCOTT
Author of 200+ Books from Self-Help and Business to Novels and Kids Books. Writer/Executive Producer of 10 Films

Gini was recently featured at a program on *Success Secrets in Everyday Life* at the Lafayette Library. Other topics she speaks about include these:

Increase Your Influence and Impact
Featuring new ways to share your message in multiple media

Increasing Your Creativity to Be More Productive and Develop New Ideas
Featuring creativity techniques, from visualization to brainstorming to using games

**Resolving Conflicts with Others and within Yourself:
at Work and in Your Personal Life**
Featuring the ERI model, based on working with the emotions, reason, and intuition to better resolve any types of conflict

How the New Personality System Can Help Your in Everyday Life
Featuring a new personality system based on discovering your Dog Type for more success in your life and work, includes visualization and interactive experience

Gini Graham Scott, Ph.D., CEO of Changemakers Publishing and Writing, is an internationally known writer, consultant, speaker, and workshop leader. Her recent books include *Success Secrets in Everyday Life*, *Increase Your Impact and Influence*, and *Self-Publish Your Book in Multiple Formats*. She has published over 50 books with major publishers and 150+ books through Changemakers Publishing on social trends, business, self-help, and for kids. She has worked with hundreds of clients as a ghostwriter for books and scripts, and as a communications strategist and consultant. Her website is www.changemakerspublishingandwriting.com.

For details: Changemakers Publishing and Writing. (925-385-0608. changemakerspub@att.net

A Flyer to Promote Future Workshops to Organizations

While you can mention your workshops in listing your speaking programs, create separate flyers for each workshop. Tailor them to either appeal to organizations that might hire you or to individuals who might attend if you are putting on the program yourself. This way you can highlight the different topics and activities you will cover in each workshop to better entice prospective organizers to hire you to conduct a workshop or individuals to attend. Here's an example of a workshop flyer I created in Word, though you can jazz up your flyer with professionally designed graphics.

SUCCESS SECRETS IN EVERYDAY LIFE
with GINI GRAHAM SCOTT

Author of 200+ Books from Self-Help and Business to Novels and Kids Books.
Writer/Executive Producer of 10 Films
Lafayette Resident for 5 Years

A Workshop on How to Apply These Success Tips in Your Everyday Life

Based on Gini's popular speaking program and customized for the members of your organizations and others who are likely to attend

During this workshop, Gini will share her secret tips on how she was able to achieve so much and how attendees can do it, too, whatever their goals, hopes, and dreams in their work and personal life. The program will draw on Gini's career experiences of over 40 years and cover topics such as:
- Turning failure into success
- Getting new ideas from one's experiences
- Setting and achieving goals
- Increasing one's creativity
- Using visualization to map out one's path to success
- Prioritizing what participants really want to do

The workshop will include discussion, interaction with others, visualization techniques, plenty of time for questions, and more.

A Brief Bio:
Gini Graham Scott, Ph.D., CEO of Changemakers Publishing and Writing, is an internationally known writer, consultant, speaker, and workshop leader. Her recent books include *Success Secrets in Everyday Life*, *Increase Your Impact and Influence*, and *Self-Publish Your Book in Multiple Formats*. She has published 50+ books with major publishers and 150+ books through Changemakers Publishing on social trends, business, self-help, and for kids. She has worked with hundreds of clients as a ghostwriter for books and scripts, and is a communications strategist and consultant. Her website is www.changemakerspublishingandwriting.com.

For details: Changemakers Publishing and Writing . (925) 385-0608 . changemakerspub@att.net

A Blog or Podcast on the Subject

Another way to build on your program is to take a topic you presented and create a blog or podcast based on it. Include a link in that to wherever you are promoting your future talks, such as a page on your website or your Facebook page.

As an example, one of the topics I described in my talk was the ERI (emotions-reason-intuition) model for conflict resolution. I might later write a blog about it describing how I applied the model to help someone having a conflict with a family member, co-worker, or boss. For a podcast, I might invite someone having a conflict with a friend or associate to do an online interview to discuss the problem and consider ways to resolve it using the ERI model.

You can also use your blog or podcast to offer something of value to your audience in order to get their email to send them various offers in the future. These offers could be for your products or services or perhaps offer an e-book or PDF with excerpts from a book you have written or are writing. Another possibility might be to offer a discount or certificate for an initial consultation with you.

A Press Release for the Local Media

You can write two types of press releases for the local media. Then, hope the editors or reporters will find this information appealing enough to include this information or contact you to write a story about what you are doing.

Start your release with "For Immediate Release" unless you are sending it to a particular editor. The two types of releases to send are these:

- a release about your next speaking gig if it's a public event after you set this up; additionally, create a short announcement to include in a calendar or newsletter mention of upcoming events.

- a follow-up release about how you are helping people in the local community through your talks on your topic, including one you recently gave.

To create a release about your next speaking gig, first determine the date and location. The goal of this release is to get individuals to know about and attend your event. Draw on the information for your flyers and announcements about the event to write the release, much like a release for your first event. But now that it is a second event, note that this is part of a series of programs you are doing on the topic.

Also in this release, you can draw attention to what you are doing to help individuals in the local community, which will provide the local media with even more incentive to cover your event and learn more about you. Additionally, highlight how you give value to others with your talks and workshops to offer another reason to feature information about you.

- <u>A Release About Your Next Speaking Gig</u>

Here's an example of a release I sent out to feature my next speaking gig:

FOR IMMEDIATE RELEASE

What Are the Secrets of Living a Longer Healthier Life Based on Interviews with 2 Dozen Seniors 80 and Over by the Author of 200+ Books and 10 Feature Films - November 2,

    For over 30 years, author Gini Graham Scott has quietly written and published over 200 books and written and executive produced 10 feature films, documentaries, and TV shows. Now she will be showing her latest film *The New Age of Aging* featuring two dozen seniors 80 and over talking about what they did to achieve a longer, healthier life. She will also discuss how anyone can prepare for such a longer, healthier life decades before. It is part of her series of talks on *Success Secrets in Everyday Life*.

    Some of these tips include standard advice for staying healthy, such as eat lots of fruits and vegetables, eat less sugar, get plenty of exercise, and keep your mind active and alert. But Gini will also introduce some of the other techniques the long-living seniors have used, such as having a pet, meditating for about 20 minutes a day, participating in local clubs, and working on one or more projects after retiring from a 9 to 5 job.

    The event is being held on Tuesday, November 1 from 6:30-8:30 at the ABC Center in Lafayette, under the sponsorship of the Living Longer Foundation.

    For more information and RSVPs, you can sign up at Eventbrite: https://www.eventbrite.com/e/success-secrets-in-everyday-life-tickets-71942956319

Or get your ticket at the door if space is available.

For more information:
Changemakers Publishing and Writing
www.changemakerspublishingandwriting.com
changemakerspub@sbcglobal.net
(925) 385-0608

- **<u>A Follow-Up Release About How You Are Helping People in Your Local Community</u>**

Here's an example of a release I sent out to seek an article about how I could help others through various activities. Likewise, when you describe your speaking program, emphasize how you help people in your community.

FOR IMMEDIATE RELEASE

Local Author and Speaker Offers Documentaries, Books, and Talks on the Secrets of Living a Longer Healthier Life Based on Interviews with Over Two Dozen Seniors 80 and Older

What should seniors do to live a longer, healthier life? What should anyone do? These are the topics a local author and speaker will be addressing in a series of programs, including a new documentary *The New Age of Aging*. It was filmed in the local area with over two dozen seniors 80 and over who described what they did to live their active, healthy old age.

Some of these tips for staying healthy are familiar, such as eat lots of fruits and vegetables, eat less sugar, get plenty of exercise, and keep your mind active and alert. But some of the other techniques the long-living seniors have used include having a pet, meditating for 20 minutes a day, participating in local clubs, and working on one or more projects after retiring from a 9 to 5 job. They also have used various stress reducing techniques, to help them stay calm in facing difficult situations.

Local author and filmmaker for over 30 years, Gini Graham Scott has begun speaking on this topic as part of her mission to help community members live more successful, satisfying lives through a variety of programs that deal with resolving conflict, becoming more creative, and better understanding the personality of oneself and others to lead to better relationship both at work and in one's personal life. To this end, she has written and published over 200 books and written and executive produced 10 feature films, documentaries, and TV shows. Now she is drawing on this past experience to offer a series of speaking programs and online courses on living a longer and healthier, as part of her series of talks and workshops on *Success Secrets in Everyday Life*.

For more information on Gini's programs and to be added to her mailing list for information on her next talk:

Changemakers Publishing and Writing
www.changemakerspublishingandwriting.com
changemakerspub@sbcglobal.net
(925) 385-0608

A Series of Short Posts for the Social Media

You can also build on your first talk by creating a series of social media posts in which you feature tips from your talk and include a link to get more information, along with a free PDF or e-book on your subject. To get it, individuals have to include their email, so you can contact them in the future.

For example, here are the first in a series of social media posts I created based on my Success Secrets talk.

SUCCESS SECRET TIPS FOR SOCIAL MEDIA CAMPAIGN

For this series, I picked out a couple of tips from the Success Secrets book, added a photo, and provided a link to the book on Amazon. Later, this social media campaign could promote the online workshops and webinars to be created.

The Latest Success Secrets Tip:

Use visualization to imagine what you want to do and how to get there. Mentally create different future scenarios for yourself. Then see what happens and how you feel about different scenarios. Once you know what you want to do, develop plans to make this happen. Want more success secrets? Over 100 tips you can apply in your work and personal relationships based on a talk series and book on *Success Secrets in Everyday Life*.

The Latest Success Secrets Tip:

To be very successful, be open to making changes along the way, so you stay flexible. Then, be ready to change your goal, your plans for getting there, or both. Every few weeks, assess how things are going and clarify if you want to stay on this path or shift your priorities, based on what is happening to you. Want more success secrets? Over 100 tips you can apply in your work and personal relationships in *Success Secrets in Everyday Life*. To get a free e-book with several dozen tips, sign up at successsecretstalk.com.

Deciding Who to Pitch

Initially, focus your pitch on your local area, since you are more likely to get your releases and announcements published. You will also be more likely to interest editors, reporters, and radio hosts who would like to interview you. Later, as you build up attendance at your events and you get more local media coverage, you can seek to get more widespread national attention. Building up your number of followers on the major social media platforms -- at least 10,000 or more on Facebook, Instagram, Twitter, and LinkedIn -- will also help you attract interest.

You can target these local contacts if you sign-up for one of the major media contact services, such as Cision or Meltwater, though these are fairly expensive for a yearly subscription -- about $3000 to $5000 a year. Thus, you need to be able to do multiple emails for it to make sense to get an individual membership, or perhaps find a partner to sign up with you. For the time being, forget about the pay-by-the-mailing press services like PR Wire, which charges $299 to send out a basic release, $199 if you get one of their 33% off promotions.

Another way to get local contacts is to gather together copies of local newspapers, newsletters, and magazines. Some of these may be freebies that appear in your mailbox, or buy a copy on a local newsstand, such as in your supermarket. Then, in each copy, look for the masthead which lists the names of the editors and reporters, and select the contacts to pitch -- generally the publisher, managing editor, senior editor, or features reporter. The titles vary, and if you aren't sure, you can call to determine who to pitch, or send an email with a letter or press release to any likely contacts. If you email multiple contacts, later you can explain you weren't sure who to send your letter or release to, so you can better target subsequent mailings.

Still another way to find local publications is by doing an online search. To do so, put in the name of your county or city along with the word "publications," "magazines," or "newspapers" to get a list of publications in your area. Besides your city, put in the name of adjacent cities. If you are near a major metropolitan area, put in that city, too. Include your state name with the city, unless you are targeting a major metropolis, since there could be cities with the same name in more than one state.

For example, when my assistant did this search, she included East Bay cities within 25 miles of Lafayette, where I am based, as well as San Francisco. Here's an example of the kind of information you get on Google -- the name of the targeted publications, a description about them, and some contact information, based on my assistants search for "Lafayette, California, publications."

Some of these publications may be members of the chamber of commerce in the cities in your area, so check with these chambers, too, for local publications. Most chambers now post their membership lists with contact information on their websites.

If you want to do radio interviews, do a search for radio stations in your area. If you want to be a guest on podcasts, search for that. For example, when I searched for podcasts in the San Francisco area, I got several listings, including one for the top ten podcasts in San Francisco.

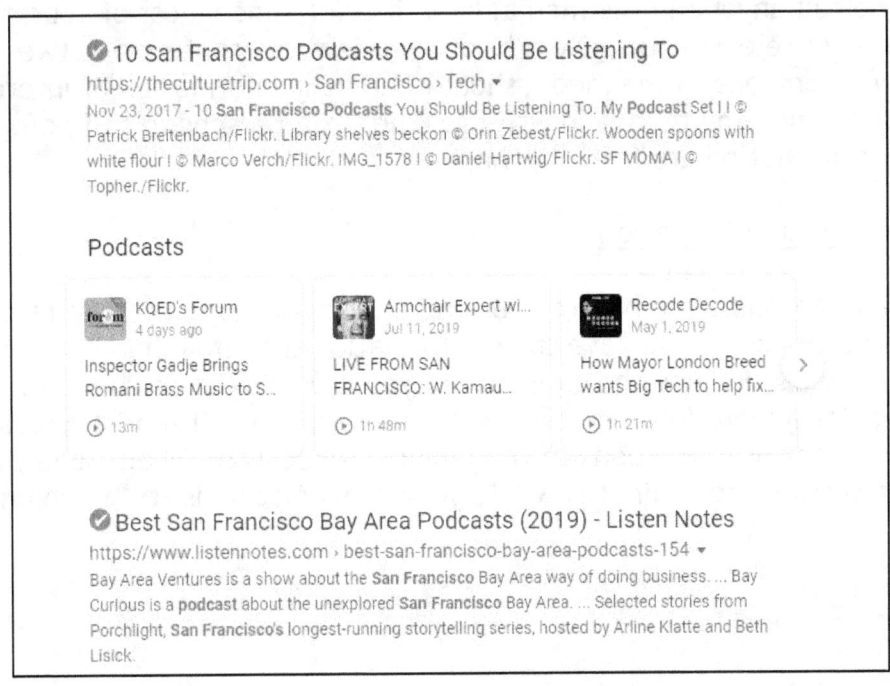

Creating a Database of Contacts

If you are creating a list of local contacts, put them in a database to use in doing bulk and personalized mailings. I have been using Access or an Excel sheet for this purpose, but you can use other database programs.

In creating this database, set up a series of columns: Number, Publication, Type of Publication, Contact, Title, City, Email, Website, and Comment, which can include the date of your data entry or update). Create another record for each contact in the database. For example, here are a few lines from the Access database I created for local press contacts.

Making Calls and Sending Out Your Pitches

Generally, people in the media prefer to receive emails with letters or press releases. Sometimes, though, it's fine to call, if you only have a small number of press contacts or if you have met someone in the media who asks you to call.

If you do call anyone in the media, keep it brief, since most of your message will be in your letter or release. Just give a brief overview in a sentence or two, highlighting why someone in the media should find your information of interest. Always plan to provide the details in writing. The main reasons to call before or after you send your information are the following:

Before You Send Your Information

The main reason to call before you send an introductory letter or release is to let the media person know you have some information they may find of interest on a certain topic. You can include the subject line you are using to pitch them. If they are interested in getting more information, let them know you will send a release or letter by email attachment or in the body of the email if requested. Then, send this information in the next few minutes, while your conversation is still fresh on their minds.

After You Have Sent Your Information

The main reason to call after you send your letter or release is to check that the media person has received it. You can recap what you sent by reading or summarizing the subject line. If they have gotten your email, fine. Tell them "great" and hang up. If they haven't received it, let them know when you sent it (sometimes the contact will check their email at this point and find it, sometimes in their spam folder). If they still haven't gotten it, tell them you will send it again, and do so in the next few minutes.

If you don't get through right away, you can leave a message and hope they get it. If you don't hear anything, follow up a day or two later. You can also follow up a few hours or a day later after sending an email to see if they received it. If they say "yes", great, and follow their lead if they want you to say more. If no, try again maybe one more time. Don't keep persisting with calls or emails, since you don't want to come across as a pest.

Sending Out Mailings Individually or Using a Mailing Service

While you can do individual mailings and phone calls when you have a small number of contacts -- say under 25, as your database grows, there are a number of bulk mailing services you can use. Some examples are GetResponse, Constant Contact, MailChimp, and GroupMail. These services can send out what look like personalized emails for letters or releases from whatever email you specify. You just enter the name of your contact and email into their software, along with your message, which can include photos or illustrations. If the service doesn't include an email server with its mailing software, you have to arrange an SMTP server, which ranges from about $9 to $15 a month for a limited number of emails (generally 40,000 a month or less). Then, you can send out these emails to each person in your database.

Commonly, you will need a .csv file to import your database records into the software to send out your mailing to those contacts. You can use Access or Excel to create a .csv file.

Should you get any returns or requests to remove an email from your database, remove it, such as using a code like "RETX" to signify a returned email and "XXX" with the reason (i.e.: REMOVE), so you won't mail to that email in the future.

For example, I have used Access for about 15 years to create a series of databases for mailings to a variety of contacts, including publishers, agents, film producers, small business owners, managers, and sales reps. After I indicate the contact's name, I export the results into an Excel file and save that as a .csv file. Next, I create a group for that data in a mail program and add my email as a recipient of the mailing to test that the mailing goes out successfully. Then, I import the .csv file into this group and add in personalizing information to the message (such as !#FIRSTNAME"! and the "email" of the contact). This way the software will insert the name on each record and send the message with the requested subject line to the contact with that email. After that, I check my email to see if I have received the message correctly (i.e.: It has been sent to my name with the correct subject line and message). If all is okay, I let the client know the mailing has gone out, and I send a PDF report with the company and contact information of those who received the mailing (though not the email, since that's proprietary).

Likewise, you can use an email server and software set-up to send out your personalized emails and use any email you want in the send and reply fields, based on your account arrangements with the company or companies providing this software and mailing.

Hiring Help with Marketing and Promotion

A final consideration is whether to do all of this yourself. If your focus is on speaking, doing workshops, consulting, producing videos, and writing books, blogs, and other materials to build your platform, learn about these different ways to expand beyond your first gig.

You probably can't and don't want to do everything yourself. While you may be good at putting on your program and developing your materials, you may not have the same expertise for doing other tasks. Moreover, you might still need help in creating your materials, such as by working with a ghostwriter or communications strategist.

When it comes to marketing and promotion, there are many detailed tasks involved in developing and producing your marketing and promotional materials and implementing a campaign. Accordingly, think about creating a team to help with marketing and promotion. You especially want people who can work with you hands-on to do the work. While a marketing or promotion consultant can help create a plan for what you might do, you need someone to do the day-to-day implementation. That way you can focus on what you really want to do and are good at.

Sometimes you may be able to find someone who can both help develop your materials, and has a team to do marketing and promotion. If not, the key people to hire include the following:

- a website designer to create your website ($70 to $125 an hour).
- a social media provider and virtual assistant to set up your social media campaign and send out your social media posts ($30 to $40 an hour).
- a publicist to contact the print, broadcast, and Internet media for you, and possibly set up your speaking engagements ($1500 to $3000 for a monthly retainer).
- a database assistant to look for contact information online and enter it into a database, such as one listing contacts for the local media, organizations or companies ($8-15 an hour).

- a marketing assistant to contact local associations, organizations, and corporations to set up speaking gigs for you ($15 to $35 an hour, depending upon experience. If someone is very experienced, you might create a commission arrangement from about 25-33% for any paid jobs they set up for you. That is about the same commission charged by a speaking bureau, although most don't actively promote you; they follow up when they have a request for a speaker on a certain topic in a certain location, or they can negotiate an agreement for you).

- a graphic designer to create your brochures, flyers, book covers, and other materials ($25 to $125 an hour).

Ideally, don't hire anyone as an employee. Rather, hire anyone as an independent contractor, which you can usually do when you have someone work for you for only a few hours a week and they can choose their own hours. Then, too, most of the people you hire will have their own businesses or work for a small business, so they will be independent contractors, not employees, for you. Hiring only independent contractors is an advantage when you are starting out, because you don't have to set up reporting systems and paperwork which is required by the different levels of government when you have an employee.

Finding the Help You Need for Marketing and Promotion

Where do you find the help you need? A good starting point is the people you already know, including family, friends, and local business groups.

Other possibilities include:

- Put a notice on your local Next Door neighborhood forum.
- Do a search on Google for the position you are looking for and add "near me" or your city or county.
- Make an announcement at any interest groups you belong to.

In my case, I found most of my team members through referrals from business contacts, and I found my database and marketing assistants through postings on a local neighborhood forum.

If you are hiring someone who is doing creative work, such as a web designer, social media provider, or graphic designer, ask to see examples of their work, which will usually be on their website. If you are hiring a publicist or marketing assistant, ask about other clients they have worked for, and if possible, see some examples of what they have done for their clients.

In the case of database assistants, I have mainly hired high school seniors and beginning college students. In the initial interview, I spent a few minutes talking to them about what they have done. Then, I asked them to take about 5 minutes to write any kind of letter, such as to pitch a product or seek a job. That letter gives me an idea of their typing accuracy and how creative they are in coming up with something to write with little direction. Finally, I invite them to work for an hour or two, since it just takes me a few minutes to explain what to do.

Taking the Next Steps

So there you have it -- an overview of how to set up your first speaking gig and build on that to take your speaking to the next level, whether you want to do talks, workshops, seminars, online courses, webinars, or other types of speaking programs.
The next step is to figure out what you want to do, plan your strategy, and implement your plan. So go to it and good luck. And have patience, because it can take time to launch this new endeavor.

ABOUT THE AUTHOR

GINI GRAHAM SCOTT, Ph.D., J.D., is a nationally known writer, consultant, speaker, and seminar leader, specializing in business and work relationships, professional and personal development, social trends, and popular culture. She has published 50 books with major publishers. She has worked with dozens of clients on memoirs, self-help, popular business books, and film scripts. Writing samples are at www.changemakerspublishingandwriting.com.

She is the founder of Changemakers Publishing, featuring books on work, business, psychology, social trends, and self-help. The company has published over 150 print, e-books, and audiobooks. She has licensed several dozen books for foreign sales, including the UK, Russia, Korea, Spain, and Japan.

She has received national media exposure for her books, including appearances on *Good Morning America, Oprah,* and *CNN*. She has been the producer and host of a talk show series, *Changemakers*, featuring interviews on social trends.

Scott is active in a number of community and business groups, including the Lafayette, Pleasant Hill, and Walnut Creek Chambers of Commerce. She is a graduate of the prestigious Leadership Contra Costa program. She does workshops and seminars on the topics of her books.

She is also the writer and executive producer of 10 films in distribution, release, or production. Her most recent films that have been released include *Driver, The New Age of Aging,* and *Infidelity*.

She received her Ph.D. from the University of California, Berkeley, and her J.D. from the University of San Francisco Law School. She has received five MAs at Cal State University, East Bay, most recently in Communication.

OTHER AVAILABLE BOOKS ON INSPIRATION, MOTIVATION, AND SUCCESS

Control Your Life, Control Your Thoughts
Pursue Your Passion
Work It Right
The Courage Book
The Gratitude Book
The Anger Book
The Forgiveness Book
The Vision Board Book
Affirming Your Success
Animal Insights
The Animal Experience
20 Rhymes for Your Success
Turn Your Dreams into Reality
The Wisdom of Water: To Your Success
The Wisdom of Water: Insights from Nature for Everyday Life
Mind Power: Picture Your Way to Success in Business
The Empowered Mind: How to Harness the Creative Force Within

CHANGEMAKERS PUBLISHING
3527 Mt. Diablo Blvd., #273
Lafayette, CA 94549
changemakers@pacbell.net . (925) 385-0608
www.changemakerspublishingandwriting.com

www.ingramcontent.com/pod-product-compliance
Lightning Source LLC
Chambersburg PA
CBHW081725100526
44591CB00016B/2504